The Agile Manager's Guide To

EFFECTIVE
PERFORMANCE APPRAISALS

The Agile Manager's Guide To

EFFECTIVE
PERFORMANCE APPRAISALS
SECOND EDITION EXPANDED

By Rebecca M. Saunders

Velocity Business Publishing
Bristol, Vermont USA

Copyright © 1998, 2000 by Rebecca M. Saunders
Second Edition Expanded
All Rights Reserved
Printed in the United States of America
Library of Congress Catalog Card Number 00-101806
ISBN 1-58099-020-7
Title page illustration by Elayne Sears

If you'd like additional copies of this book or a catalog of books in the Agile Manager Series™, please get in touch.

- **Write us:**
  Velocity Business Publishing, Inc.
  15 Main Street
  Bristol, VT 05443 USA

- **Call us:**
  1-888-805-8600 in North America (toll-free)
  1-802-453-6669 from all other countries

- **Fax us:**
  1-802-453-2164

- **E-mail us:**
  action@agilemanager.com

- **Visit our Web site:**
  www.agilemanager.com

The Web site contains much of interest to business people—tips and techniques, business news, links to valuable sites, and electronic versions of titles in the Agile Manager Series.

Contents

Books in the Agile Manager Series™:

Introduction

Both employees and managers dread performance appraisals.

On one side, employees worry that they may be the victims of arbitrary opinions or unclear expectations. Much is at stake, they know, including raises and promotions.

On the other side, managers don't like to sit in judgment of others, particularly when those others are employees whose co-operation and support are necessary to bottom-line success. Most managers can't forget, either, that they may wind up in court if a disgruntled employee complains of discrimination to the Equal Employment Opportunity Commission or to a lawyer.

A good appraisal system relieves the pressure on both sides. When objectives are clear and set by managers and employees together, and when they jointly monitor progress toward them, fair and accurate appraisals are almost guaranteed. Good workers get the recognition they deserve, and poor performers learn about problems before they grow out of control.

Clear objectives and careful monitoring—that's what the appraisal system you'll read about here is all about. It's also a great way to manage employee performance. With it, you provide coaching and feedback over the course of a year to raise employee productivity and address subpar performance.

In this system, the final, year-end appraisal is a written conclusion to a year of performance management. It's easy to produce, because you keep careful records throughout the year. And it's friendly to employees, because it focuses on strengths rather than weaknesses.

This is the kind of appraisal system that management theorist Peter Drucker and other experts seem to favor.

In his book *The Effective Executive*, published in 1963, Drucker observed that the appraisals of that time focused "on a search for faults, defects, and weaknesses" and measured employees on "potential" rather than on performance.

More than thirty years later, many appraisal programs continue to focus on weaknesses rather than strengths. They are still based more on "potential" than accomplishment. Not so the appraisal system proposed in these pages.

Further, this system, because it's based on clear objectives, will help you sleep easier. For one thing, your appraisals will be defendable, both to higher-ups in your organizations and in the courts.

More important, it will give you the opportunity to direct employees toward your department's or company's mission, and it provides a firm foundation for decisions about pay raises, promotions, transfers, or terminations. And, maybe most important, it builds and sustains good relationships between you and your employees.

Note: All aspects of employment are legal minefields these days. Because every company's situation is different, and because laws differ depending on where you are, it's important to have an employment attorney familiar with local laws assess your appraisal program before you implement it.

The Productive Appraisal

Chapter One

Use the Right Approach To Appraise Performance

The Agile Manager, feet on desk, looked glum. Appraisal time again, he thought, staring at the file folders in front of him. Great.

He looked upon performance appraisals as a necessary evil—something to satisfy the human resources department and avoid legal trouble. I'd still be a good manager without them, he thought—or an even better one, because I'd have more time. And I wouldn't be forced to point out the faults of an otherwise good person.

Wanda, his second in command, bounced into the office. "Hi," she said. "Ready to go over the appraisals?"

"I suppose," he said in a flat tone.

Sensing his lack of enthusiasm, she said brightly, "You know, these can be quite useful. I've turned people around through appraisals."

"Really? I never have."

Seeing an opening, Wanda said, "You could—but we'd have to use more of a results-based system than what we now use."

"What do you mean?"

"Well, in my last job, we had a system that . . ."

There is usually a right and a wrong way of managing most things, and performance appraisals are no exception. If you don't do them right, you can lose out on the many benefits the appraisal process provides. You also waste valuable time, since conducting appraisals is a time-intensive activity.

What You Need from an Appraisal System

These questions highlight the most important aspects of any appraisal system:

- Does the appraisal system produce information that is relevant to the job and consequently legally defensible?
- How accurate is the approach in measuring performance?
- Does the system allow you to compare different individuals with the same job in different sites within the organization?
- Will the system enable different managers presented with the same observations or data to reach the same conclusions?
- How useful is the performance information gathered? Can it be used to coach or counsel an employee or otherwise improve performance?

What's Out There

Let's look at some common appraisal programs and how they address these issues.

The Narrative Approach. In this method, you write essays that answer the question, "How would I evaluate this employee's performance over the past year?" Generally, the narrative approach does not require that you justify your assessment.

The value of this method depends on the observational, memory, and writing skills of a manager. The assessment may be accurate and relevant—or not. There is no real way of making a judgment because no one sets guidelines that allow you to compare the performance of one employee against another employee in the same position.

Different managers presented with the same situation might rate an individual the same way, but if you haven't reported specific incidents in the narrative, there is no telling how another manager might assess the same employee.

Further, the conclusions themselves may or may not provide direction for coaching or counseling the employee. Again, it depends on your skill as a writer and what you include in the narrative.

How does the narrative stand up to the legal test of objectivity? Since there are no standards or objectives—just the opinion of one manager about one employee—the narrative is not legally defendable.

Trait Rating. In this approach, you rate your people based on traits like good interpersonal skills, creativity, dedication, or teamwork. Courts look askance at trait rating. Part of the problem is that the traits rated are often broadly defined, as are the criteria for rating the level of performance associated with the trait.

Equally difficult to defend is the job relevancy of the traits being measured. It's easy to let your feelings about an employee influence the rating.

Besides, some traits are hard to define, like the ability to collaborate or network. Such traits might be critical to employees doing their jobs well. But if they are to be useful guidelines, you have to translate them into behaviors that can be measured.

Recently, organizations have begun to measure how well employees practice corporate values, which can be equated with traits. But because companies often don't identify values with job-relevant behavioral norms, problems arise. This leads to complaints from employees about unclear expectations: "What do you mean I'm not innovative? What, precisely, do you expect?"

Unclear expectations also make it unlikely that different managers presented with the same observations or data would reach the same conclusions.

Without clear ties to behavior, the values themselves don't translate into any action steps that managers and employees can take to improve an employee's performance.

360 Assessments. This is one of the newest approaches to appraising employees. It's based on traits, but it translates them into behaviors and skills first. Then it rates the importance of the skills and behaviors in a job and how successfully the job holder practices them.

Employees rate themselves and are rated not only by their immediate supervisors but by peers, subordinates, other managers, and even customers. (That's a full circle of people, hence the name "360.")

For instance, managers might be rated on their ability to "Focus on customer needs," "Build relationships," "Foster teamwork," or "Value diversity."

Under "Focus on customer needs," specific skills might be: "Aid customers to identify the best solution to their needs," "Meet commitments to customers," and "Seek feedback from customers."

Valuing diversity might be based on a manager's ability to "Confront prejudice and intolerant behavior," "Champion the promotion of employees from diverse backgrounds," or "Create an environment that is not hostile to people with diverse backgrounds."

Most 360 assessments are used to evaluate managers. Since several people are drawn into the process, taking 360 appraisals down to the ranks would make it exceedingly time-intensive for the organization. And there is some question about the subjectivity of the assessments. It's easy for people being assessed to influence the assessment by selecting friendly peers to evaluate them. A manager's boss, also, needn't substantiate his or her assessment. That could make an evaluation suspect in the eyes of the court.

At present, most 360 assessments are used to help people develop professionally rather than for personnel decisions like raises or promotions. The proponents of 360 assessments, however, advocate their use for these purposes as well.

Management by Objectives (MBO). This method has been used for many years to evaluate employees as well as set corporate goals and develop action plans for achieving them.

As an appraisal tool, MBO enables manager and employee to set a group of specific goals together and measure and evaluate the employee's performance against it.

Critical to the legal defendability of MBO-based appraisal systems is the wording of the goals. They need to be clearly defined and measurable, so that what constitutes achievement is clear. Consequently, managers can't punish employees with a goal like, "produce better quality widgets." However, they can ask employees to "decrease the amount of rework on widgets by 10 percent by adhering better to customer requirements."

The Benefits of Results-Oriented Appraisals

Of the various systems just described, the one you'll read about here is closest to an MBO or results-based system.

It is a five-step process of managing performance that continues throughout the year:

- Step 1: Set goals or objectives.
- Step 2: Observe and monitor performance.
- Step 3: Share observations with employees.
- Step 4: Evaluate annual performance and institute a plan to develop employee skills and abilities.
- Step 5: Set new objectives.

In addition to the usual year-end review, you meet formally with an employee three other times a year. In these quarterly meetings, you have an opportunity to chart progress on goals, provide needed coaching or skill-building, reassess the goals, and more.

You'll also meet with employees frequently on an informal basis and make a point of documenting critical incidents—those that highlight on-the-job strengths and weaknesses.

Done well, the payoff for your work is a humming, productive department of dedicated workers that make you look good.

We'll describe this system in detail in the coming pages. But first let's see how it fares based on the questions raised at the start of this chapter:

- *Does it produce information that is relevant to the job and thus legally defendable?* Yes. When you set goals that are aligned with organizational and individual effectiveness, assessments become job-relevant and are legally defendable. Best, the system provides direction for employees.
- *How accurate is the approach in measuring performance?* You base assessments on concrete results, which are easily measurable.
- *Does the system allow you to compare different individuals with the same job in different parts of the organization?* Assuming that each job holder has the same objectives, you can compare performance based on the results each achieve. Different individuals, even in the same jobs, might have different strengths, so results-based evaluations allow you to play to individual strengths.
- *Does the system enable different managers presented with the same observations or data to reach the same conclusions?* Obviously yes. The results determine the assessment.
- *Can the information at the end of the year be used to coach or counsel an employee or otherwise improve performance?* Yes, it can. But manager and employee must work together to identify the reasons behind the failure to achieve a goal.

The next chapter gives you an in-depth overview of the appraisal system.

The Agile Manager's Checklist

✔ Be prepared to spend time on appraisals. Nothing is as useful in measuring and improving employee performance.

✔ Set measurable objectives that link to the aims of the department and organization. Worthwhile objectives get more buy-in by employees.

✔ Avoid focusing on personality traits or values without behaviors tied to them.

Chapter Two

Know the Performance Appraisal Steps

"*Five steps? That's a lot of work, isn't it?*" The Agile Manager, having shaken off his lethargy, was now sitting up straight with his feet on the floor.

"*It's managing,*" said Wanda with a smile. "*It's what we're paid to do. And if you manage the process well, it saves you time, because you build on strengths and never let anybody slack off.*"

"*Hmm. I like this the more I hear about it. Let's give it a try—we don't have anything to lose.*"

"*Excellent,*" said Wanda, happy to be teaching the Agile Manager something important for once.

Let's look at each of the five steps in our results-based appraisal system.

1. Set Goals or Objectives

In the first step of the process, you meet with employees to set job-related goals or objectives. Most are tied directly to departmental or organization-wide performance goals. They are often "hard" objectives like sales quotas or productivity targets.

They may also be departmental or companywide values, also

called "performance factors." More and more, organizations are looking for evidence that employees "show respect for one another," "innovate," "show integrity at all times," or "are responsive to customers." It's important, however, to tie these values to meaningful on-the-job behavior. Otherwise they become empty phrases.

Besides performance factors, you and your employees will set developmental objectives based on weaknesses or untapped potential highlighted in the past year's performance appraisal. These could be a part of an effort toward advancement and growth or improvement in skills.

Goals are normally set at the start of a new year. Starting with a clean slate on January 1 has psychological value. But feel free to start your "new" year anytime, especially if your company always holds annual reviews, for instance, in the fall.

In the meeting, you pick five to eight objectives or factors to track. Some are critical to effectiveness within the job, others impact the organization's strategic goals, and some pertain to an employee's development. Others reflect corporate values.

Then you'll prioritize and weight each item for importance and difficulty, and (probably) set a deadline for its completion. The form you fill out (see page 32) becomes the basis for discussion at each quarterly review.

Goal setting is best done in a dialogue between you and your employees. You need to prioritize goals and agree on reasonable deadlines for achieving them. Otherwise, you are unlikely to get employees to "buy in" to the goals set.

2. Observe and Monitor Performance

If employees are to meet goals, it's important to monitor their efforts to achieve them. You observe and offer feedback, and you create a written record of important events in an employee's work life, both good and bad.

In observing an employee, you aren't only developing documentation for the quarterly interviews that are part of the appraisal process. You should be prepared to provide daily feedback, if called for, to help employees achieve results.

While the program includes formal interviews to review performance with employees, you don't wait for one of them to praise good effort or begin problem solving. Praise can encourage even greater effort, and attacking a problem early can eliminate the need to bring it up during the next formal meeting.

Besides observing progress in achieving results, watch that employees adhere to values that are important to the department and company. You want evidence that your employees are practicing the values your organization espouses, be they teamwork, "synergy," risk taking, good customer service, or what have you.

Best Tip

Don't wait for quarterly performance reviews to either praise good effort or begin solving a problem.

3. Share Observations

Over twelve months, you will meet at least four times with each of your employees to discuss performance during the past three months. The most important of these meetings is the fourth—the year-end review.

The purpose of the interim interviews is to clarify any expectations that remain unclear, set plans for the next quarter to ensure continuation of current progress or get the employee back on track, and leave both you and the employee in agreement about the employee's performance for the year to date.

These sessions also let you remind employees about the department's goals or broader, corporate values.

The basis of discussion in these meetings is the list of objectives you prepared together at the start of the year. To support your comments, you will have with you a written record of observations.

Each time you meet, you update the objectives form. Most forms have, like ours, space for comments. At the bottom, there is space for your initials and those of your employee to indicate you have shared your conclusions with the employee.

You may not have enough room to write all your comments.

In that case, you may want to write each quarterly review on a single sheet of paper, initial the sheet and have the employee initial it, and attach the review to the form.

Why schedule formal sessions? Companies recognize that their managers are very busy, and consequently that they may not be giving ongoing feedback. Formal meetings, as part of an appraisal system, ensure managers give their people regular and timely feedback on performance.

Admittedly, this process consumes time. The more direct reports you have, the more time-intensive the review process is. Consequently, more and more companies are reducing the number of reviews during the year—from the usual four times a year to three or to as few as two.

Quarterly reviews are also the basis for defendable decisions about an employee's year-end evaluation should a disgruntled employee take the company to court and argue that a negative evaluation came as a complete surprise.

They also give you a chance to reinforce comments made during the work day.

4. Evaluate Annual Performance

At the end of the year, you and your employee meet to evaluate the employee's work over the previous twelve months.

Ideally, the annual review covers two meetings. During the first, employees share their accomplishments with you. You listen and praise where appropriate and raise concerns where justified.

For instance, say Don promised to conduct a market study over the course of the year. He's done the study, but his weaknesses in planning and researching make some of the data questionable.

On the other hand, the survey identified some key customer needs that could develop into profitable products. Don needs to be praised about the opportunities his work revealed but he also needs to be cautioned about the care he gives such studies.

At this meeting, your objective is not to evaluate Don rigorously but rather to engage in a productive dialogue with him, one that sums up his performance over twelve months. You emphasize the objectives set at the start of the appraisal year.

You want the employee to leave feeling that there was an open and honest communication between you. If there were problems during the year, you level with the employee about them. Likewise, you work to create a climate in which employees feel comfortable enough to admit shortcomings. Your goal is to ensure that your evaluation, which you will share with the employee during the next meeting, won't come as a surprise.

Between the first and second meetings, you complete a numerical appraisal (you'll read all about it in chapters three and eight), compute the final rating for the employee, and create a narrative evaluation to go along with it.

In the second meeting, you share this document with the employee. You also bring to the meeting various records and documents that influenced your final rating.

Best Tip

In every meeting, you want the employee to feel there has been honest, constructive communication between you both.

If you have been honest with the employee throughout the year-long appraisal process, the final rating should come as no surprise. Reviewing the form together also helps you and the employee identify gaps in skills, abilities, and knowledge.

You then have the employee sign the appraisal form, not necessarily for approval but to confirm that the appraisal meeting took place.

This meeting is also when you'll probably want to discuss raises, bonuses, and other compensation issues. Some companies, however, wisely decouple appraisals and salary reviews. This removes an element that might otherwise distract either the manager or the employee during the meeting.

Some companies also hold off discussing dollars for administrative reasons. They want to make sure all the paperwork has been processed so an employee gets a promised raise promptly.

Finally, you use the appraisal to identify areas in which training or coaching might help the employee improve or excel in the coming year.

5. Set New Objectives

Soon after the year-end appraisal, you sit down with your employees to set objectives for the next year. If any employee encountered problems during the past year, the objectives for the coming year should include some developmental goals.

So the process goes. And it is what occurs as a consequence of this ongoing process that makes this method of appraising employees most beneficial to you and your organization:

- Employees learn about their strengths along with their weaknesses.
- Employees actively participate in both the goal-setting and evaluation process. That, you'll find, empowers them.
- Employees are recognized as individuals and know their manager is concerned about their needs and goals.
- Employees have a better sense of their fit within the department and company as a whole. You and the employee become a team of two working toward a common, agreed-upon organizational mission.

The Agile Manager's Checklist

✔ Set goals that reflect the department's mission and corporate values.
✔ Let your employees collaborate to set mutual goals.
✔ Reinforce corporate values and the departmental mission daily, at periodic interviews, and at the annual appraisal.
✔ Use an employee-development plan to fill gaps in knowledge within the team and department.

Lay the Groundwork

Chapter Three

Set Useful Objectives

"Now let's consider William," said the Agile Manager. "His main job, as I see it, is to oversee the introduction of about twelve products—including those with enhancements—every year. That averages three a quarter."

"Right," said Wanda, "but there's more. He also helps out on writing product manuals, and he's always the one who supervises interns in the department."

"Can we quantify those things?"

"The manual part is easy—let's say he helps out on four manuals a year. And remember, we run that figure by him to make sure it's both fair and doable."

The Agile Manager nodded and said, "And as far as the work with interns—any ideas?"

"The most important thing is that they don't get in our way," said Wanda, laughing. "He does a good job of that. But let's talk to him about making sure they contribute to the department—giving them quantifiable goals, even if they do work for a pittance."

"As for developmental goals," said the Agile Manager, "I'd really like to see William learn a bit more about finances. It'd help him make better presentations, for one thing. For another, he might

stop and think about how his proposals affect the bottom line."
   "HR has a course in understanding financial statements," said Wanda. "Is that good enough?"
   "It's a start," said the Agile Manager.

Establishing good performance objectives is the foundation of the appraisal system. It's not only a way to provide fair and accurate performance appraisals; it's also a way to help employees achieve departmental plans and corporate goals.

First: Identify Key Results

Our appraisal system measures performance against predetermined, verifiable objectives. These objectives are based on aspects of the employee's job that contribute most to the overall success of the job and that offer the greatest benefits to the organization.

To come up with objectives, therefore, start by looking at job descriptions and department or corporate plans. You should also look at last year's performance objectives.

These goals should become a means of measuring your employees' performance over the year, so you should:

- Define the specific end results in clear and unambiguous terms.
- Set timetables for each goal if you can.
- Ensure that the objectives will be feasible given department resources.
- Be sure you can measure the progress toward objectives in some manner.
- Select objectives that support the tactical or strategic objectives of the organization.

Your performance measures should demand some employee stretch.

Admittedly, the more "stretch" you put into an objective, the more resistance you'll encounter from an employee. But don't let this discourage you from setting objectives with some challenge. Just be sure that the stretch is realistic. Too much stretch means that objectives won't be feasible, and employees won't even try to achieve them.

Set Goals and Performance Factors

Objectives come in a few different flavors. Let's take a look at the most important:

Performance Goals are results that, achieved, make an employee effective.

For routine jobs, they might also be called *standards*. These are usually numerical and tied to output. Standards are also the same for each employee in the same job. For instance, a standard for copy editors might be: Edit no fewer than ten manuscript pages per hour. For a customer service rep: Process no fewer than forty orders weekly.

Wherever you can, set standards that apply to all employees in a category. Example: Every shipping clerk must pick and pack fifty orders a day.

How do you come up with standards? Look at historical data on how productive other workers have been doing the same jobs.

The less structured the employee's job, the more the goal reflects an accomplishment or implementation of a new process or procedure. For instance, a market researcher might have as a goal, "Set up a process to get feedback from sales reps." Or a goal of a quality engineer might be to "Implement a program to monitor scrap levels by July 31 to save the company $1 million." A salesperson might have this goal: "Open up twenty new accounts in Omaha by June 15."

Developmental Goals reflect skill, ability, or knowledge deficiencies that need shoring up. An employee might lack statistical know-how, for example. His goal: to "complete a course on statistical analysis by the end of the year." Another might have poor presentation skills. Her developmental goal: to "put together a presentation for client firms following completion of a six-week community college program on public speaking."

The goal doesn't have to be tied to a course. An employee might have something like this as a goal: "Read *The Effective Executive* by Peter Drucker and identify five ways you can apply the knowledge to interactions with colleagues. Deadline: March 31."

A *Performance Factor* is different from a goal. It reflects behaviors based on things like corporate values. Consequently, managers may have little discretion about what they are. However, managers do have control over how they are defined in relation to employees' jobs and how they are measured. That's important, because without some method of measurement, performance factors are meaningless.

Best Tip
Weight your list heavily with concrete, reachable objectives. Keep performance factors to a minimum.

For example, a performance factor for everyone in a company might be to show "initiative." For a department administrator, that could be defined as "Develop a user's team to increase clerical workers' knowledge of new software program."

For an engineer, it might be defined as "Identify less expensive ways to manufacture existing products to increase profit margin."

If the performance factor is "collaboration," you could measure it by an administrative assistant's ability to "fill in when colleagues are either ill or away on vacation." For the engineer, collaboration might be measured by her ability to "participate fully in cross-functional projects so they are completed on schedule."

Performance goals are less difficult to justify legally than performance factors. Results-based objectives also provide the best direction for employees, making clear how they can contribute most productively to the department's and company's efforts.

For those reasons, weight your list heavily with concrete objectives and keep factors to a minimum.

Consider Dream Objectives for Outstanding Employees

You may have employees who need more challenge than others. Perhaps these employees have plateaued in their positions and need opportunities to "work outside their boxes." Yet they might also need direction about how they should use their talents. Discuss a "dream list" of objectives with them off the record.

The dream-list objectives are goals above and beyond those you've listed in the appraisal form. They are just between you and the employee.

A dream list objective for an administrative assistant might be: "Develop a procedural manual for the department." For a product manager, it might be, "Identify a product extension and develop a business plan for consideration by

Best Tip

Give your best employees 'dream' objectives that will help them learn to work and think outside the box. You'll all benefit.

the firm's new-product development committee."

The employee must agree not to pursue these grander objectives until all other key results have been achieved. In turn, you must agree to recognize the employee's accomplishments through mention in the appraisal, a special "performance memo," or extra compensation. But don't promise a large raise or big bonus unless you can fulfill on that promise.

Word Objectives Effectively

The next step is to write out the objectives. Begin with an action verb, describe the immediate results if necessary, include the date by which you want the goal achieved, and define the overall result desired (in terms of quality, quantity, increased sales or reduced costs, or some other factor). The formula:

---

                                                                     by

(action verb/result)

_____ in order to_____.

(timetable)   (key result area)

For example: Establish a work group to investigate a market for health-related cereal products and complete a report by January 1 in order to expand our product line.

Another: Review office procedures by July 15 to identify ways to streamline operations.

Still another: Hold weekly staff meetings beginning June 2002 to improve communications among department members.

Meet and Get Buy-in

Often managers set objectives, then present them to employees as a *fait accompli*. While employees may agree to such objectives, it's unlikely that they will buy into them and work toward them with dedication.

The most effective goal-setting process is one that involves the employee from the beginning. Write down prospective goals for employees, but then sit down with them to discuss the list.

Even better, encourage some or all employees to come to the goal-setting meeting with their own objectives. Those closest to the work often know its goals as well or better than you do, and you do them honor by asking them to participate in setting yearly objectives. It can also be an excellent method to better engage indifferent workers in their jobs.

> **Best Tip**
>
> Always, always, always discuss the list of objectives with employees. It's the only sure way to get 'buy-in.'

It's an interesting exercise for both you and the employee to set objectives independently, then meet to compare and agree upon them. Even if the employee is way off base in what he thinks is important, it's a good opportunity for you to help him see the big picture.

Weight the Objectives

Once you and the employee have worded the goals, transfer them to a form like the one on page 32 (and feel free to enlarge it on a copier and use it yourself). Now it's time to weight the goals in terms of difficulty and importance. You'll base your year-end evaluation on your weightings of each goal.

Measure both difficulty and importance on a scale of 1 to 3, with 3 being the most difficult.

The level of difficulty reflects not only the individual's ability, but how hard the goal will be to accomplish. Importance is based on the objective's impact on job success or department or corporate mission.

A goal with a 3 rating in importance may have a difficulty rating of 1, 2, or 3. Likewise, a goal with an importance rating of 1 may have a difficulty rating of 1, 2, or 3. If you have done a good job of identifying goals critical to the success of the job or department or company, most of your goals should have an importance rating of at least 2.

You should also determine what percentage of the final evaluation each goal will represent.

The mathematical process is simple: First, multiply the level of difficulty by the level of importance of each goal. Add the products of each.

Next, to determine how much the achievement of each goal will impact the final rating, divide the product of each goal by the sum of the products.

Here's an example with five goals:

Goal	Importance		Difficulty		
Goal #1	3	x	2	=	6
Goal #2	3	x	3	=	9
Goal #3	3	x	3	=	9
Goal #4	3	x	2	=	6
Goal #5	1	x	3	=	3
			Total		33

Objectives	Impor-tance	x	Diffi-culty	To-tal	_____ Quarter, 200_
Performance Objectives 1.		X			
2.		X			
3.		X			
4.		X			
Development Objectives 1.		X			
2.		X			
3.		X			
Performance Factors 1.		X			
2.		X			
Additional comments:					Initials:____Employ ____Manag Date:____

Performance Appraisal Form

for _____

Goal #1 represents 18 percent of the final rating (6/33). Goal #2 represents 27 percent of the rating (9/33). And so on.

Determine the levels of importance and difficulty together with employees. If they have had input into decisions about how much impact each goal will have on the final rating, it is less likely that they will contest it. And point out how completing one goal and failing to complete another might influence the final rating.

Once you have all the goals weighted and prioritized, have the employee sign or initial the form. That signifies that he or she agrees with them.

Be Numberwise

Note that we suggested from five to eight objectives and performance factors. You wouldn't want fewer than five for an employee; there wouldn't be sufficient challenge. Nor would you want many more than eight. In that case, employees might disperse energy in too many directions. If you find yourself exceeding eight items on the list, see if you can't postpone some until the upcoming year.

The objectives you choose may change during the course of the year. Sometimes, circumstances outside either your control or the employee's will eliminate one or more. There may also be a need for a new objective during the twelve months, and you may have to replace one less important objective with the new one.

Be flexible. The system will bend with you. Encourage the employee to comment on the existing goals and whether any of those set at the beginning of the year should be lowered or crossed out and new ones set to replace previous ones.

Best Tip

Be flexible with objectives. Circumstances may change and you may have to reprioritize the list, or you may need to add objectives.

The Agile Manager's Checklist

✔ Set results-based objectives and have your employees set their own, then meet with each employee to reach agreement on the final goals.

✔ Set goals based on jobs, not based on individuals holding the jobs.

✔ Set from five to eight objectives.

✔ Set realistic objectives but ones that require stretch.

✔ Prioritize and weight the objectives to calculate their impact on the overall rating.

Chapter Four

Document Employee Performance

The Agile Manager buzzed Wanda. "What's this 'Performance Memo' you sent me on Anita? You could've just told me how well she did on the Moran project." The Agile Manager hated unnecessary paper.

"That's something that goes along with our appraisal system. I think I told you how important it is to document behavior along the way," she added coolly.

"You did," said the Agile Manager. "So Performance Memos are part of the documentation?"

"Yes—and it goes in her file to support whatever ratings we give her in performance reviews."

"Ah, I get it. You gotta be patient with me, Wanda old buddy. I'm used to storing such information in my brain, not a file cabinet."

"Smart as you are," she said with a slight smirk, "there's no way you can remember something that happened six months ago unless it was extraordinary. And you're probably like most of us: You remember what happened in the past few weeks—good and bad— and believe that's what the employee's been like the whole year. With good documentation, you can put the employee's yearly contribution into much more useful perspective."

"Thanks professor," he said. "And by the way, I really do appreciate the education. It's clear I need it."

Contrary to what some managers believe, you document performance for reasons beyond protecting yourself from charges of discrimination. Good documentation also ensures you conduct an accurate and effective appraisal discussion.

For instance, you may have an employee who has done a spectacular job on a team project but a mediocre job otherwise. Without documentation for the entire year, you might give her a rating higher than deserved.

It works the other way, too. You might have a hard worker who makes one major mistake just before the annual appraisal. Without documentation, you might let that one error overshadow a year's worth of quality work.

Documenting performance is also a means of pinpointing an area for improvement. You can point to an incident that shows specifically what an employee is doing wrong.

Telling an employee her "handling of customers is poor" isn't enough. But if you can tell her that on several instances you observed her "losing her temper with customers" or "socializing with co-workers while customers waited to be served," or "providing inaccurate product or price information to customers," you can start her on the road to improved performance.

The more specific the information—time, day, circumstances—the better.

Don't Make Excuses

Many managers may believe in documenting employee performance in theory, but many don't practice it. Among the excuses managers use:

- **I have a good memory.** Maybe you do, but most people remember most clearly things that happened within the last few weeks. To conduct productive quarterly reviews, you must be able to look at performance over the last three months. To do an accurate annual appraisal, you need to consider an individual's performance over twelve months. Can you count on your memory to recall each critical incident that should influence the final rating?

- **I don't have the time.** Managers have never been busier than they are today. But documentation need not take a lot of time if you create forms like those in this chapter and use them regularly to record information.
- **I could write something that could put me in legal trouble.** So long as you focus on job-related facts, you should have no reason to worry.

Document Critical Incidents, Problems, and Successes

Good documentation consists of keeping two kinds of ongoing records:

Incident reports. These document specific events, including actions taken by the employee and the results. (Some astute managers call these critical incidents. It's a way to remember not to bother recording the trivial.)

Employee Incident Form			
Employee:			
Position/Grade:			
Salary:			
Date	Event	Action	Result

Progress reports. These reports evaluate employees' problems and successes as they work on team projects or other ongoing assignments. They can also be used to record any training the employee has taken or incidents that over time suggest a shift (either for good or bad) in performance.

These records are for you alone, unless an employee disputes your review and you need to show your documentation.

Useful Memos

You'll also have occasion to employ two other documents, both designed to share with employees.

Performance memos. If you want to alert employees to a problem, or commend them for a fine job, produce a "performance memo" like the one shown on the opposite page. Give it to the employee and place a copy in the employee's personnel file.

Even if you're commending good performance in the memo, don't make promises. That is true throughout the appraisal process, but especially when you write anything down. These include records you keep for your eyes only. The employee or a

Employee Progress Report		
Employee:		
Position/Grade:		
Salary:		
Date	Nature of Project/Training	Assessment (Problems, Successes)

Performance Memo

To: Hal Crawford
Job Title: Materials Engineer
From: Jim Schmidt, plant manager
Date of Event: July 18, 20XX
Event: Last Friday, you informed me that you had contacted a vendor to discuss the raw materials our firm has been receiving from him. Because of some problems with previous shipments, you suggested a tour of the supplier's facility. During that visit, you identified several problems with their products that have cost us considerable time and raised quality issues about our own products.

Together with the supplier, you developed an action plan that, once implemented, should reduce production time by 10 percent and reduce product defects by as much as 15 percent.

I commend your initiative, and I will pass a copy of this memo along to Lisa Stratton, senior vice president/manufacturing.

---

third party may one day be in a position to see the record.

Warnings. If there is a clear performance problem, and discussing it with the employee has led to no change in behavior, then you may want to issue a warning memo to the employee and place a copy in the file. Unless your organization has a form to use for warnings, use a standard memo format, identifying as the subject of the memo "Written Warning." (See page 40.)

If an employee is involved in an altercation or other situation that requires disciplinary action on your part, you may want to have the employee read the documentation you've prepared and sign it to show that he or she agrees with the facts as stated. This

---

Written Warning

To: Thomas Hartshorne
From: Jill Pulaski
Subject: Your Lengthy Lunches

Last month, we discussed the matter of your frequently extended lunch periods. This was not the first time I had discussed your practice of taking more than an hour for lunch. We've discussed it on three previous occasions.

When we met yesterday, you explained that you had been running errands for your wife, who can't leave the house because of a broken leg. You promised that, in the future, you would not go beyond your lunch hour unless it was absolutely imperative. If it was, you said you would ask my permission and plan to stay late to make up the time. I trust you will keep your word.

You must show improvement in this area during the next three weeks. Otherwise, you will be subject to disciplinary action, including suspension. At the end of three weeks, we will meet again to review the problem.

---

will protect you and your company from an employee's accusation that you misinterpreted the situation.

Finally, take notes on the quarterly appraisal meetings you have with employees, especially when you're assessing poor performance. Note what you said, the response, and plans for action.

What to Document

What should you record? Certainly not hearsay ("Tim says Gina is starting to drink at lunch time"). Nor should you include opinions, even your own. ("I don't think John has what it takes to work here long-term.") Your conclusions may be justified, but as a valid record they mean nothing.

With good documentation, a third party reading the record will come to the same conclusion you have. This is possible only when you provide detailed descriptions of specific incidents and facts.

Besides, nine months after you entered a comment like, "George did a poor job of working with vendors," would you recall what George specifically did wrong? You need to record facts like these:

- "George did not send specs to the vendors in time to get the client's approval before work began on the Jensen project."
- "George failed to keep the vendor informed of client changes, and he sent a number of spec sheets to the vendor with errors. As a result, the company lost about 20 percent of anticipated revenue from the job."

Other don'ts:

- Don't document rumor. You shouldn't use it to evaluate an employee, so it doesn't belong in your incident or progress reports on your employees.
- Don't include personal comments about an employee, including judgments about hairstyles or how "good" or "bad" they appear or dress.
- Don't include documentation about events that are not behavioral, such as when

Best Tip

Don't document hearsay or opinions. Document concrete successes, skills learned, problems solved, and lapses in professional conduct.

a colleague tells you that your employee is "lazy." Rather, write something like, "According to Fred Hanover, Hannah has refused to lend a hand to colleagues faced with tight deadlines. She completes her work then sits and waits for the next assignment rather than seek out work." The problem with words like "lazy," "introverted," or "argumentative," whether your comments or another's, is that they can show prejudice or bias. Consequently, they should be kept out of your employee reports.

Document the Facts

The most important things to document are your observations of actions and results. But you should also include observations from other managers who have worked with the employee on projects in which you were not involved.

What if the employee works in another location and you have infrequent opportunities to observe the individual at work? Then you must depend on the observations of other people. This is especially true when employees spend most of their time dealing with people in other departments or with those outside the company.

Keep a record, then, of remarks from customers or clients or others outside the firm.

Also, note when employee performance impacts the output or jobs of others and how their behavior has done so—good or bad.

Following these rules can ensure that you do fair and accurate appraisals of your employees——and prevent accusations of arbitrary and capricious decisions.

Manage Your Records

Create macros or templates on your computer for all the documents discussed here. It'll save you time. Many office networks now have "personal information management" software that allows you to set up reports similar to those shown in this chapter to record critical incidents and employee progress.

Since it shouldn't take more than a few minutes to update these reports weekly, use a notebook if paper and pen are more your style. The most efficient way to document your employees' performance is to set aside a convenient time during the week and mark your calendar. Friday afternoons are often a good time, say from 3:00 to 5:00, when the week is coming to a close.

Most record keeping can be done weekly, but record special incidents as soon as possible.

The Agile Manager's Checklist

✔ Maintain personal logs on each of your staff members, not just problem workers.
✔ Update personal logs regularly.
✔ Document based on facts, not hearsay.
✔ Date and detail critical successes and failures.
✔ Where a serious problem has occurred, like a rule infraction, write up the incident as soon after as possible. Have the employee sign the written record.
✔ Document discussions of problem performance.

Interlude One

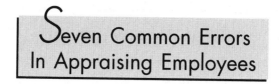

Seven Common Errors In Appraising Employees

You can follow a well-planned appraisal program, but your success still depends on execution.

Managers commonly make seven errors in putting an appraisal program to work:

- They set poor standards of performance.
- They fall prey to rating biases.
- They don't allow sufficient time for the appraisal process.
- They spend more time talking than listening to the employees they are appraising.
- They don't document employee performance. Or they do keep records, but they aren't valid for fair and accurate appraisals.
- They rate everyone's work as satisfactory.
- They don't include an employee-development or follow-up plan.

Let's look at each of these errors in greater detail.

Define Standards of Performance

Too often, the objectives aren't clear to either the employee or manager, or both. Sometimes the manager sets standards or goals without input from the employee. Sometimes the manager takes a cavalier attitude toward goals and hands a list to the employee without clarification. Sometimes the manager and employee talk to one another but don't truly communicate, because each talks in generalities.

For example, a manager may ask an employee to improve "quality" but not define it. What happens? The manager tells the employee, "You really haven't improved the quality of your work." The employee responds, in turn, "How can you say that? I shortened the time it takes to process orders and I've increased the accuracy of data entry. What else did you expect of me?" Manager: "That's not what I meant by quality. I wanted you to . . ."

To avoid confusion, standards and performance goals must adhere to the SMART model. They must be:

- **Specific.** They must state specifically what must be accomplished.
- **Measurable.** They must be quantifiable (for example, put in terms of cost savings, productivity improvement, or profitability).
- **Attainable.** They may require "stretch," but they should be within reach.
- **Realistic.** After discussion, both you and the employee have to believe that the objectives can be attained. If an employee has doubts, hear him out. Together you may find a way around the problem.
- **Time sensitive.** Set a date by which the objective or outcome will be achieved.

Avoid Biased Thinking

Rating biases can benefit employees or hurt them. Biases thus come in two forms—the "halo effect," and the "horns effect."

Halo biases can be due to:

Overemphasis on recent performance. Rather than consider the entire year's performance, many managers let one recent positive incident influence the twelve-month evaluation of the worker.

Overemphasis on one situation. Even though it might have happened at the start of the appraisal year, one good event overshadows a generally lackluster year.

Overall likability of an employee. When a manager likes a worker, she may get a good evaluation despite mediocre performance.

Horns biases are attributable to:

No forgiveness. An employee began the year poorly but then turned the performance around. Yet the manager fails to recognize the change, letting past mistakes blind him to the significant improvement in work.

Prejudice. A manager lets a personality conflict with the employee overshadow performance.

Grouping. A manager rates employees who associate together similarly despite differences in the levels of their performances. A good employee who associates with mediocre or average employees tends to be rated like members of the clique.

Indiscrimination. Here, either no one gets a good rating or everyone does. The manager is either too easy or too hard on employees.

Stereotyping. Race, sex, color, religion, age, or national origin blinds the manager to the quality of a person's performance. (While we assume that the conclusion is an unfavorable assessment, stereotyping can also create a "halo effect," blinding the manager to a worker's faults.)

How can you minimize the halo and horns effects? Follow the appraisal technique this book suggests.

Don't Rush Through Evaluations

Although we all know that a great deal rests on appraisals, many managers don't give enough time to the process. Not only do they rush through the paperwork, maybe even completing it minutes before they meet with employees, but they speed through meetings as well.

Managers with tight calendars may forgo discussion entirely.

They hand a completed appraisal form to an employee and say, "Read this and sign it, please." That communicates to the employee that they regard the performance appraisal—and therefore performance management—as a mere formality.

As a result, employees don't feel the need to change their behavior. What's more, if an employee disagrees with the assessment, it may lead her to refuse to sign the appraisal, demand to see the supervisor's own manager about the appraisal, or even seek out a lawyer if the appraisal means no promotion or threatens job security.

Doing a good appraisal demands thought, concentration, and many hours spent over the course of the year. But it really pays off in improved performance and fewer management headaches.

Let the Employee Talk

During appraisal interviews, you should speak no more than 20 percent of the time. Let the employee talk the remainder of the time.

You may think you know all you need to know to do a fair evaluation of your employees, but you can't be sure unless you give your workers the chance to share their views about the jobs they are doing. If a problem exists, the dialogue may also help you to get to its cause.

Document, Document, Document

Documenting a worker's performance is important at all times to support an evaluation. It is essential if you are criticizing that performance. The employee is unlikely to accept your evaluation unless you can refer to specific incidents and cite what happened, when it happened, and the consequences of the event.

While you may have discussed a situation right after it occurred, and provided feedback throughout the appraisal period, it is amazing how an employee will have forgotten all about it by appraisal time. Your written records will serve to remind everyone what happened and when.

Treat Employees as Individuals

Some managers rate everyone's performance the same—average. Others go even further and rate almost all their employees above average or outstanding.

Why? They may lack information to justify a rating of poor work. Or they may consider a satisfactory rating the safest, least confrontational way of handling appraisals. Or they may see their employees' assessments as a reflection of their own work as supervisors—and believe that only poor supervisors beget poor workers.

But classifying everyone's work as satisfactory or better deprives good workers of the recognition they deserve and poor performers of the information that might help them turn their performances around.

Managers don't get off any better, either. Falsifying the facts only loses them credibility with bosses who are more likely to believe their own observations of a manager's staff than the manager's evaluation.

Be honest in your assessments. Good documentation can justify poor evaluations, and while a few of your employees may be deaf to negative feedback, continuous communication with your workers ensures that most know where you stand about their work.

Follow Up on the Appraisal

Follow appraisals up with employee-development efforts to eliminate the weaknesses that your evaluations identified. The development effort could be remedial, or it could be designed to move a superstar off a plateau and enable him to advance within the organization.

Discussing the development effort with an employee also lays the foundation for discussing next year's standards.

Fruitful Appraisal Meetings

Chapter Five

Prepare and Meet

"Item #3," said the Agile Manager glancing at his clipboard. "'Improve understanding of finances by taking a class.' How you doing in that department, Willie?"

"Well, I haven't taken it yet. But I plan to."

"When?"

"I'm kinda busy right now with the 3300 project. Once that's done, I'll sign up for a class."

The Agile Manager reached for a brochure on his desk. "The HR department sent me this list of classes. Understanding Financial Statements is offered only twice more this year—starting July 15 or September 15." He looked at Willie expectantly. "Which will it be?"

"Maybe I could do it next year," said William. "I'm real busy, and I have an extra intern this year."

"You committed to taking the class 2½ months ago, remember? You agreed you could use it." The Agile Manager, while cordial, was in no mood to let him off the hook. "I need you to learn that stuff. You'll be more valuable to me—and to yourself."

"But I don't—"

"'But me no buts,' as my father used to say. If you don't want to

51

take one of the classes here, find another one. Remember: It's one of your goals for the year."
"Yes," said William sullenly.

If you're to accomplish all you expect from appraisal interviews with your employees, you must prepare for each session. You have to give your employees an opportunity to prepare, too.

Be Clear About Your Objectives

You want to accomplish five things during quarterly performance reviews with your employees:

1. Discuss and agree on the quality of the employee's performance.
2. Identify strengths.
3. Identify areas for improvement.
4. Create an employee-development plan if improvement is needed.
5. Agree on your expectations (what's to be done and how) by the next review.

Note: The year-end appraisal, while sharing most of the characteristics of the other three, has a few special concerns. See chapter eight.

Don't Rush the Session

Given your objectives, and their importance, set aside an hour or more for each quarterly employee interview. Expect to hold one or more follow-up meetings with some employees to accomplish items 3 and 4 on the list above.

No matter how many meetings you hold, be sure that each is free of interruptions. If you work in a cubicle, hold the meeting where your conversation won't be overheard, like a conference room. If you have a private office, make sure you aren't interrupted.

Wherever you locate your meetings with employees, make

sure that everyone will be comfortable. These meetings can be uncomfortable enough without hard chairs and tight quarters to make you and your employee antsy.

Be Ready

Given the importance of appraisal interviews—developmental and legal—these are sessions that you shouldn't try to "wing."

If you plan to meet in your office, move the papers off your desk so they don't distract you from the discussion. A clean desk also suggests to employees that your mind is totally on them during this period.

Move the visitor's chair close to yours, to add to the employee's feeling of ease.

Of course, more important than arranging the physical location is organizing the information and materials you will cover during the interview.

Be sure you have all the documents you need for the meeting, especially performance memos

Best Tip

Take time before the appraisal meeting to make a plan for conducting it and to go over your objectives.

and the critical-incident report. The flow of the discussion might be disturbed, and never regained, if you have to stop to locate an important piece of paper.

Plan to focus on the employee's performance and the facts of that performance. Use a yellow marker to identify a couple of the items on the critical-incident report that illustrate a point you wish to make or an idea for improving performance.

Structure the Meeting

Before the meeting, you also need to think about how you will begin it. Consider your employee's interests. Maybe it would pay to start the meeting by talking about sports or weather, or the employee's family.

If you are known to get right down to a matter, it may even

be better to do just that. If people don't associate you with small talk, it may unnerve them. In that case, get down to business. Begin with some statement like, "Terri, we're here to discuss your progress since our last interview. How would you rate yourself since then?"

Best Tip

Use the sandwich format for the meeting—begin pleasantly, get down to business, and end on a high note.

However you begin, your goal should be to create a positive climate for the discussion.

Also think of an overall structure for the meeting. Among the options:

The Sandwich Format. One approach to discussing performance is the "sandwich format." Contrary to popular belief, the sandwich approach does not entail first praise, followed by criticism, followed by more praise. Rather, the sandwich format means beginning and ending the interview on a positive note. The opening remarks put the employee at ease for the meeting. The closing comments leave the employee feeling that you have faith in his or her ability.

You might say, "It's been a good year, and you've made some major improvements to help eliminate the problems we have been having with customer service."

Then in the course of the interview, you mention some continuing problems with customer service, like not getting back to customers quickly enough or typing names in wrong.

Then you both address the problems and how to avoid them.

At the end of the session, you close the meeting by telling the employee, "We have never had such good relations with customers. I think that has a lot to do with your good work. Thanks very much."

The Problem Session. Alternately, you might approach the meeting as a problem-solving session. You can begin, "There are a number of problems I'd like to talk with you about." You then identify the specific problems and discuss with the employee how those performance gaps can be corrected.

The Checklist Approach. Use the appraisal form itself to structure the meeting. Go down each item one by one. (See the example on the next page; note that the objectives have been shortened to fit.) Write your comments in the last column as you go.

Whichever approach you take, be sure to give your employees time to prepare for the meetings, too. They'll need to assess their actions in the past quarter and, perhaps, come with new objectives or suggestions of their own. When you set up the meeting—at least a week in advance—tell them to be ready to discuss their performance, as well as any other concerns.

Meet with the Employee

Invite the employee in and go through the preliminaries you decided upon.

Once you get down to the business of the meeting, ask the employee for a self-assessment first.

Listen to the employee's list of accomplishments over the appraisal period, then ask the individual what he or she would identify as strengths and what he or she would consider areas needing improvement.

Then it's your turn—but remember that the meeting is a dialogue, not a monologue or a chance to rant.

With the agreed-upon objectives and performance factors in front of you, cover problem areas or work your way down the list. After discussing each item, identify further steps that need to be taken to achieve the goal.

If you have observed some negative incidents related to achieving an objective, bring them up. But focus on one or two at most. You want to look toward future job improvements, not dwell on past mistakes.

If this is the year-end review, don't give your evaluation before you've given employees the chance to talk about what they have done over the last quarter. If you jump the gun, you'll

Performance Appraisal Form
for Gladys Rudwan, Customer Service Rep

Objectives	Impor-tance	x	Diffi-culty	To-tal	2nd Quarter, 2003
Performance Objectives 1. Increase # of calls handled to 20/hour.	3	x	3	9/ 20%	Calls now average 17/hour. Gladys needs to learn how to end calls faster.
2. Work with sales reps to create a customer feedback form by 6/30.	3	x	2	6/ 14%	First meeting held; mission set; first draft of form due before next review.
3. Reduce data entry error rate from 20% to 5% by 12/31.	3	x	3	9/ 20%	Errors at 18%. We expect significant improvement by next quarter.
Development Objectives 1. Become more familiar with product line by attending product introduction meetings.	3	x	2	6/ 14%	Has attended one meeting and missed one (not her fault). Plans to rearrange schedule to ensure availability.
2. Become familiar with data-entry system by attending in-house training session.	3	x	1	3/ 7%	Has completed training.
Performance Factors 1. **Initiative:** Alert callers to new products to increase sales.	3	x	3	9/ 20%	Call monitoring shows Gladys is making an effort to upsell.
2. **Teamwork:** Partici-pate in product devel-opment team meet-ings to share insights.	2	x	1	2/ 5%	Meetings held after 5 p.m., making attendance impossible. Will prepare written reports instead.
Additional comments: Gladys continues to improve in many ways. Next big step: Reduce data entry errors.					Initials:GR Employee MS Manager Date: April 12, 2003

create an extremely negative climate. Employees won't say a word and, for that matter, won't think it worth their time to do so.

Praise good work and its contribution to the department's plans sincerely. When you must point to problems in performance, make clear by word and tone that you are raising these issues not to condemn but to improve future performance.

As employees discuss what they have done to date, take notes. You don't want to forget new commitments, goals, or achievements.

Prepare for a Second Meeting

After you and the employee have covered goals, work yet to be done, strengths, and potential problem areas, you should have some idea how you will proceed.

Sometimes, a second meeting is called for. It's more work, but remember: The more you help a worker improve, the easier your job becomes.

For instance, you may want to write your conclusions and review that document with the

Best Tip

Make sure the employee knows that your criticisms aren't meant to condemn but to improve future performance.

employee at a follow-up meeting. Or you and the employee may decide to use a second meeting to determine areas for improvement and the actions the employee will take between the meeting and the next review.

For example, you might say, "Chris, we've found a few areas where we should be moving ahead faster. I'd like you to identify one such area and come back next Tuesday with your suggestions for how we can make better time, OK?"

At this follow-up meeting, your goal is to get agreement not only on the need to change but the plan to change performance.

Some Points to Remember

Scan this list just before your meeting.

Explain the purpose of the interview. If need be, review as well the reason for the performance-appraisal form. Workers have seen the appraisal process used vindictively or to justify preordained personnel changes. Explaining the purpose of the process and how it will be conducted reduces hostility and sets the stage for cooperation.

Focus on performance, not personality. You can discuss initiative, carefulness, integrity, and the like, but discuss them in relation to the job. Cite specific examples of job performance that reflect these traits.

Best Tip
Explain to the employee how you arrived at your conclusions. Show your documentation if necessary.

Don't become confrontational. There may be differences of opinion, but don't let them erupt into angry words.

Don't use your position to pressure the employee. You're the boss. That means that employees have to listen to you. But it doesn't guarantee that they will buy into your opinion and respond accordingly. If you assert your authority during the meeting, you could lose the rapport so important to a frank discussion.

Consider showing your documentation to the employee. If an employee questions the review, be prepared to show documentation or notes you take during the meeting.

Keep salary issues out of most discussions. This is a topic that you shouldn't discuss until the year-end appraisal, after you have completed the final evaluation.

Explain your evaluation. Let employees know how you came to the conclusions you have reached to date. If they are based on observations, say so. If you got feedback from others, let them know that, too, although you need not name names.

Refer to your initial assessment as tentative. Make clear that you are willing to change your midterm appraisal if the employee can convince you that you are wrong. Never be afraid to admit a mistake. And let them know they can change your opinion for the better before the year-end evaluation.

Send a constructive message. End the meeting with a warm handshake if it seems comfortable. Or just say, "Thanks for coming in. I feel that this was a profitable discussion. I know that I can count on you in the future. I'll be here to help you if you need it."

Mean what you say. Don't let that parting remark be an empty promise. Be available to help the employee make improvement a reality.

Remember to have the employees initial the form and give them a copy. Doing so provides reinforcement for your words.

The Agile Manager's Checklist

✔ Find a quiet place and allocate sufficient time for a real discussion.

✔ Do your homework. Review goals, critical-incident reports on the employee, and other documents before the meeting.

✔ Have some icebreakers in mind to start the meeting on a positive note.

✔ Arrange the room in which you will meet to ensure good rapport and a good exchange of information.

✔ Give employees enough advance notice to prepare their own record of accomplishments for the meeting.

✔ Plan how you will conclude the meeting or the transition to a follow-up meeting in which you discuss specific improvement efforts.

Chapter Six

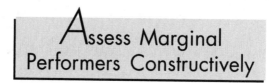

Assess Marginal Performers Constructively

". . . and as a result, the documentation isn't getting to the printer on time." Wanda relaxed her shoulders and let Manuel speak.

"Yeah, well, it's William and Anita too. Why aren't they being singled out?"

Completely defensive, Wanda observed. "This conversation is about your work, Manuel, not theirs. And I'd really like to hear what you have to say about it. This isn't a disciplinary meeting— it's about how to get jobs out the door more quickly."

"Well," said Manuel, "we could start by talking about getting a new workstation. There are three of us trying to use the desktop publishing software all at the same time. And that software's a big problem, too. I can do simple stuff, but the harder things throw me. And another thing . . ." Wanda let him continue for another five minutes.

"OK," she said finally. "We can't get another computer workstation, at least not for another year. One thing we can do is get some software training for you. How does that sound?"

"That'd be a good start," he said. He seemed happier, more like his old self, having unloaded.

Wanda continued. "And I hear you saying that you're having trouble working with people at times—"

"Not people," said Manuel. "Person. William, to be exact."
"What are we going to do about that?"
"Fire him?"
"Not funny. I have a couple of options. I can change your job around a bit so you interact with him less, or I can . . ."

Good news is easy to communicate to an employee. Everybody likes to be able to say, "Your performance has consistently exceeded expectations."

Bad news is much harder to deliver: "I'm sorry to say that your performance has been substandard through the year." Ouch.

It isn't only goof-offs or those with poor attitudes who fail to meet the standards or achieve the key results or outcomes you need. Among other reasons outcomes aren't achieved include:

- A lack of resources to make things happen
- Work that doesn't match the employee's abilities
- Training gaps
- Employee carelessness.

Where probing identifies the problem, and you believe the situation can be remedied, then the discussion about the staff member's performance may not be easy on either of you. But it can still have a happy ending if you employ the right employee-development program.

What if you have tried and tried and performance still continues to be marginal? Then you may have to alert the employee that his job is in jeopardy.

The employee's first reaction to the news will be defensiveness. Maybe he will disown responsibility: "How was I supposed to know there was a problem about how I did my job?" The employee may try to shift the blame, play dumb, or argue that he was powerless under the circumstances.

Prepare to Defend Your Evaluation

Sometimes the employee will go so far as to deny the existence of any problem, no matter how often you discussed it.

Consequently, you should have with you at the appraisal interview the following documentation:

Your critical-incident and progress reports. Use a yellow highlighter to identify those incidents that confirm your assessment.

Performance memos. If the performance is bad enough for you to consider firing the person, then you should have performance memos and/or warning notes about the staff member's work in your personnel file. They prove that you have raised these issues with the employee before.

If you lack this documentation, then you need to ask yourself whether you have done a good job making clear the seriousness of the situation to the employee. If you conclude that you haven't been as forthright as you should have, then use this meeting to level with the employee, documenting it to support any decision you may have to make in the future.

> **Best Tip**
>
> Make clear what the employee must do to meet your standards, and by when.

Standards, key results, or outcomes expected of the employee. These are the goals set by you both at the beginning of the year. Using the records you have kept of the employee's performance, read specific examples of how the problem performer's work has not met the standards set. If the employee argues that the agreed-upon results or outcomes were unrealistic, counter the complaint by pointing to other employees within your department who had similar standards but met them. If that is not the case, remind the employee that over the year you have both discussed the performance factors and/or objectives.

Be Specific About Changes Needed

Besides reviewing the employee's poor performance, let the employee know what changes you expect, and by when.

If you've discussed these performance problems before, be as clear as possible about what the employee must do to salvage the job.

Don't just say, "I expect you to improve." Be specific. Set short-term goals for the employee and agree on a timetable of future meetings to discuss the employee's progress in achieving them. If the employee thinks it will help, be willing to give her closer supervision as she makes the effort to improve.

The Long and Short of It

You may want to set long-term goals with employees, as well as short-term ones, to demonstrate your faith in their ability to improve if they try. But be honest with employees about the consequences if they don't change. Don't hesitate to let them know when they've reached the point at which their jobs are in jeopardy.

Leveling with employees is not only fair to them. It is critical to protecting yourself and your firm if a fired employee takes legal action. The employee should not be able to testify that the termination came as a complete surprise.

Don't Make Judgments

If an employee's problem is attitudinal, you need to be more careful in discussing the situation than you might if the individual were chronically late or made careless mistakes regularly.

Don't tell the employee, "You have the wrong attitude for this organization." Be specific. Discuss the behavior that is causing his performance to deteriorate and its consequences on workflow. Remember, appraisals need to be job-related and behavioral in nature.

If the employee's attitude is bad, use examples to show how the behavior has a concrete, negative impact on operations.

For example, Delores, a customer rep, is short-tempered, especially when customers ask lots of questions. To improve

Delores's attitude, you tell her that customers have complained about how hard it is to get product information from her. You point out that, as a result, some have bought from competitors instead.

In each case, your documentation backs up your assertions. That allows you to be blunt. "Your behavior suggests that you don't like doing the work that you do. If that is not true, you will need to change the behavior."

Stay Calm in the Face of Emotional Outbursts

Employees' emotional responses run the gamut from tears to shouts to threats of violence.

Some employees may do nothing more than listen silently, then walk away. While this quiet hostility can be unnerving, the more outwardly emotional the reaction, the more difficult it will be to deal with.

If employees cry in response to your criticism, offer some compassion, along with tissues and time to compose themselves. Suggest a second meeting later in the day.

Employees sometimes attribute the situation to a previously undisclosed personal problem or illness. They may argue that they need some kind of special accommodation from you.

Best Tip

Because some employees will dispute your view of things, keep documentation handy. Support your assertions by discussing specific incidents that led to the meeting.

Demonstrate your concern but don't let this sudden revelation distract you from the purpose of the meeting, which is to get the employee's performance back on track. Even people with personal problems or something covered by the Americans with Disabilities Act must do their jobs. But hear the employee out and together come up with an action plan that ensures the necessary change in performance will be forthcoming.

Let Employees Blow Off Steam

If the employee grows angry and starts to shout, don't reciprocate, even if you are the target of overflowing anger. Stay calm while the employee blows off steam. Until she has had a chance to vent, she won't be ready to talk about the situation with you.

And don't interrupt. Any comment you make until the employee is done will only escalate the anger. It suggests that you aren't interested in an explanation. Rather than interrupt, maintain eye contact. Lean toward her to show you want to hear what she has to say.

Best Tip

If you feel threatened in the least, call in a fellow employee immediately.

When the employee pauses for a moment, acknowledge that she has the right to feel as she does. Summarize what you have heard to verify that you've understood.

Let the employee wind down. Once she has regained control, propose that you both develop a short-term action plan that could reverse the situation. If she still seems unable to control her temper, offer to continue the discussion later.

Protect Yourself

Sometimes an employee will become so angry that he threatens you or promises violent acts against the company. If you feel threatened, call security. If you work for a small company, call in a co-worker.

Even if the situation doesn't develop to the point that you feel in danger, report the threats to either the human resources department or your immediate supervisor. If you have to fire the employee, have a third person in the room, maybe even a security person nearby, should he try to carry out his threats.

Today, unfortunately, the number of violent acts within companies by disgruntled employees is growing. You dare not take a threat lightly.

Be Prepared for the Silent Glare

The exact opposite of the angry employee is the clam, an employee who listens to the news and then silently leaves your office, unwilling to discuss the issue further.

Generally, this behavior is attributable to the employee's emotional reaction to the news. It is so strong that the employee feels she would be unable to keep her emotions in check. Talk to the employee later, once she has calmed down. But sometimes the clam hides in her shell, refusing to speak further about the issue. You may then have to demand a meeting, whether the employee wants to talk out the problem or not.

Best Tip
Try to draw out employees who clam up. Getting them to talk is an important part of improving performance.

Variations of the clam are employees who listen but continually try to change the subject to avoid the final conclusion—that they could be terminated.

Then there are the employees who try to rush through the discussion, exhibiting unease by tapping their foot or drumming their fingers, maybe trying to distract you by pointing to other tasks that aren't getting done while the two of you are meeting. These people are trying to hurry you through the interview so you can't emphasize the points you had planned to make.

Sometimes an employee you expected to become defensive will start to shout, then suddenly regain control of her emotions, agree with your assessment, then get up to leave.

It would be great if you could go along with the ploy, but you can't. You haven't gotten through to the employee or accomplished the goal of the meeting.

In these and all other cases, stick to your guns. You need to start a dialogue with the employee in the hopes of salvaging the situation.

You're not done until you and the employee have identified

possible solutions and agreed on short-term goals that the employee must meet by a certain date.

If the employee needs to get used to the idea that action must be taken *or else,* then give that person the time. Schedule a second meeting to get down to work counseling.

Record the decisions you reach at the final meeting and have the employee sign the document. You'll need this record if the effort proves as fruitless as previous efforts to turn the employee's performance around.

The Agile Manager's Checklist

✔ Come with documentation to defend your evaluation of the marginal performer.

✔ Don't let the employee's behavior distract you from the purpose of the interview.

✔ To get buy-in to the remedial action plan, involve the employee in the planning.

✔ Include follow-up meetings to monitor progress toward achievement of the goals.

✔ Be clear about the consequences of not improving performance—and also how you define "improvement."

✔ Don't let this meeting change your relationship with the employee. You can be accused of making it impossible for the employee to turn performance around.

Chapter Seven

*F*air and Legal Appraisals

"I just wanted you to know," said the Agile Manager, "that Manuel's been making noises about discrimination concerning your meetings with him."

Wanda froze. "No! How could he? I've got tons of documentation and—"

"Hang on," said the Agile Manager. "I know you do. And I know you don't have a discriminatory bone in your body, not with all you've been through to get where you are."

"Damn right." Wanda, the fear passing, became angry.

"Here's my assessment of the situation," continued the Agile Manager. "Manuel is a bit of a blowhard. He's tried to pass off responsibility for bad results a few times over the years. When I've mentioned it to him, he gets even more defensive. But he always seems to get the point and then tries to do better."

"So what's the next step?" asked Wanda.

"It's your call. If it were up to me, I guess I'd sit tight to see if it passes. I'm guessing it will—and that your words will have the right effect on him. Besides, you're clear legally with all the documentation you've been keeping, not to mention the constructive advice you've given him . . ."

Performance appraisals can influence compensation, promotion decisions (and the opportunities to gain promotions through training or a high-visibility assignment), layoffs (employees identified as poor performers often head the lists for downsizing), and termination for cause. Consequently, appraisals are targets for legal action by disgruntled employees who charge bias in your evaluation or the way you implement the appraisal system.

Avoid Three Legal Traps

Most lawsuits related to performance appraisals are based on the failure of a manager to:

- Follow the program's procedures consistently;
- Have sufficient documentation to support evaluations;
- Be objective in assessments by applying criteria consistently.

1. Follow the same procedures with every employee. Imagine that policy at your organization calls for quarterly reviews, but you review one employee only once at the end of the year. You give that person a poor rating and no raise. Maybe you even put the person on warning.

He may have a case for contesting the appraisal because he, unlike his peers, didn't get the benefit of ongoing feedback and consequently can claim he had no way of knowing a problem existed.

Best Tip

Apply your appraisal program's procedures and standards consistently. That's often enough to fend off lawsuits.

If the situation is serious enough to warrant termination, the employee might sue, charging that the oversight was deliberate and attributable to a personal animosity or an age, race, gender, or other bias.

2. Support evaluations with documentation. It's easy to contest an appraisal when it doesn't point to specific incidents, and when it is filled with empty sentences like "The employee is unable to follow instructions," or "The employee doesn't have the motivation to do the work."

The disagreement can wind up in court. There, you will be expected to prove your case by citing specific incidents in which the employee failed to perform to standard or didn't meet objectives.

Until recently, companies settled many of these cases out of court. Even if the company knew that a manager's decision was the right one, the potential cost of a high damage award, the legal fees associated with a trial, and the embarrassing publicity often made it more sensible to settle out of court.

But, as companies have learned, out-of-court settlements can trigger more and more frivolous lawsuits. Many now take a stand. They aren't as willing to give into legal blackmail if they can provide compelling arguments in their defense.

Best Tip

Never forget: Your goals and standards must be job-related. You can't give poor reviews based on untapped 'potential.'

This change in thinking places a heavier burden on you, the manager, to provide an adequate paper trail for evaluations of employees. It protects you and your organization.

3. Be consistent in the application of standards. Evidence that even one employee was allowed to get away with a situation that led to termination of another employee can be sufficient to win a court case.

Let's say an African-American was late 75 days during the year and was ultimately terminated for chronic lateness. Study shows, however, that even though you fired a few other employees, white and black, for the same reason, one white employee with over 75 latenesses is still working in your department.

The lawyer might argue that the black employee might not have been terminated had he been white. And the plaintiff might win his case at considerable cost to your employer.

Consistent application of standards across staff can be proven one way: through careful documentation.

Evaluate on Goals, Not Potential

The court will also investigate your goals and standards to be sure they are realistic and based on the actual needs of the job. This is required under the Equal Employment Opportunity Commission's Uniform Guidelines on Employee Selection.

The Guidelines demand that standards be "valid," or job-related, and, beyond that, that your firm's appraisal system measures job performance accurately.

These rules mean you must evaluate on objectives alone. You may have a very talented individual who fails to use her full potential. You may know that she is capable of doing much more than the standards set. It may be frustrating to see her let that potential go to waste, but as long as she is meeting the standards you've set, she is doing the job.

Avoid Documentation Traps

Courts question managers who can produce documentation only about poor performers or have only bad things to say about an employee. Critical incidents, good and bad, should be documented for all employees—poor, average, and outstanding workers.

Too much documentation can backfire, too. It provides more fertile ground a lawyer can plow to dig up an instance of discrimination. On the other hand, extensive documentation discourages frivolous lawsuits. Unless a lawyer sees potential for a high damage award, he or she is unlikely to invest valuable time digging for evidence of unfair treatment of a client.

Know the Law

Given these potential legal traps, it's no wonder managers dislike doing appraisals. They worry that they might trip over some legal technicality even when their assessments are just and accurate, and when they have gone out of their way to treat all staff the same.

To protect yourself, stay abreast of legal developments. That includes decisions in court cases that might impact the law. Then you are less likely to make the wrong move.

Best Tip

Stay abreast of developments in employment law. Ignorance in this area can be costly or even sink your company.

In particular, know six major employment laws and keep an eye on court cases related to them:

Title VII of the Civil Rights Act. This act makes it illegal for an employer to discriminate against an employee in hiring and promotion practices because of the individual's race, color, sex, creed, or national origin.

The Equal Pay Act. This act stipulates that employees who perform similar jobs must be paid equally.

The Age Discrimination in Employment Act (ADEA). This act protects employees and applicants more than forty years old. It states that employers may not discriminate against individuals in this age group in either hiring or promotion decisions.

Section 508 of the Rehabilitation Act. Employers cannot discriminate in hiring or promoting the handicapped.

The Vietnam Era Veterans Readjustment Assistance Act. Under this act, companies with contracts of $10,000 or more with the U.S. government must take affirmative action to employ and advance in employment qualified disabled veterans and veterans of the Vietnam era.

The Americans with Disabilities Act (ADA). This act makes it illegal to discriminate in hiring, in job assignments, and in the treatment of employees because of a disability. It doesn't affect evaluations directly, but it does cause managers to worry when they are giving a poor evaluation to someone with a disability. Could it land them in court? The answer: maybe, but probably not. The law doesn't allow disabled individuals—no matter the disability—to get away with not doing their jobs. But every reasonable effort must be made to accommodate the employee's work to the disability.

There have been, of course, new developments with these laws, including amendments and court decisions, that managers also need to be aware of.

For instance, since passage of Title VII of the Civil Rights Act, overt workplace discrimination has decreased. Courts now look for subtler signs of discrimination, like the existence of code words that demonstrate a hostile environment for plaintiffs.

In *Aman v. Cort*, two black employees sued their employer, claiming that they had been subjected to an atmosphere of racial contempt and harassment. Blacks at the firm were referred to as "another one," "one of them," and

Remember: Laws like the ADA and Title VII cover all phases of employment, from hiring to separation.

"poor people." The company controller, in talking to one of the two plaintiffs, made a remark to her about "all of you" that he refused to explain.

The court found for the plaintiffs, noting that "antidiscrimination laws and lawsuits have 'educated' would-be violators such that extreme manifestations of discrimination are thankfully rare." But, the court continued, discriminatory conduct still persists. It is just that racial intent is now often masked.

Be Sensitive

Besides knowing the law, it's important to be sensitive in communicating with employees. You can often avoid complaints of unfairness, even charges of discrimination, from employees who didn't like what they heard during the appraisal by maintaining a positive exchange.

And watch that you don't say or think something about a person that reflects upon membership in a protected group.

For instance, Jed is over sixty and his performance has been slipping recently. You suspect he is having a problem using the new office technology. You shouldn't say to him, "Jed, I know at your age it's hard to keep up with the new technology, but . . ."

You may think you are being understanding, but the remark could be seen as an unfavorable response to Jed's age.

Better to keep your remarks neutral. Level with employees in terms of their performance, but do everything possible to avoid saying anything that could give the appearance of prejudice or discrimination based on race, color, religion, age, sex, national origin, or veteran's status.

The Agile Manager's Checklist

✔ Maintain ongoing communication with the employee. Information you share during an evaluation should not come as a surprise to the worker.

✔ Make a written record of any discipline meeting with an employee, particularly if you don't expect the behavior you discussed to improve.

✔ Have supportive documentation to justify your ratings or evaluation.

✔ Be specific and support your evaluation with hard facts.

✔ Stay up to date on the legal technicalities.

✔ Be sensitive when communicating to avoid saying something inadvertently that might be perceived as discriminatory.

Interlude II

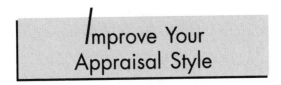

Improve Your Appraisal Style

Your appraisal style is a mixture of three factors: assertiveness, listening skills, and probing ability. Each helps you conduct productive appraisals and get top performance from employees.

Learn to Speak Up

Despite the training programs companies offer to build managers' skills in appraising performance, many supervisors and managers are still ambivalent about telling employees that they aren't doing the job they want done—even during an appraisal interview.

How about you?

Do you bring problems up in an assertive manner during appraisal meetings, or do you give satisfactory ratings regardless of performance?

It's dangerous to stay silent about performance issues. If you do, circumstances may one day trigger an emotional response in which you dump your pent-up feelings on an employee. You rant and rave rather than address the problem in a calm, collected way.

At the time you blow up, the employee probably isn't doing anything worse than she has done before. But it's not her actions that trigger your response. Rather, it is the circumstances you are in when you observe the employee violating a rule or otherwise not pulling her weight on the job. Your emotions are at a peak—maybe you have a desk piled high with papers and the phone is ringing off the hook. The misbehavior is the last straw.

The employee likely doesn't even know that there is a problem, because you have been so good at keeping it from her. When you take your pent-in emotions out on her, she might ask, justifiably, "What am I doing wrong?"

Why don't a lot of managers level with employees about performance during appraisal interviews?

- **They fear a confrontation.** They want to avoid it at all costs—even employee productivity. After all, their parents taught them, "If you don't have anything nice to say, don't say anything."
- **Employees might not like them anymore.** They don't want to lose their staff's friendship or not be accepted by employees.
- **They don't want to hurt an employee's feelings.** Criticizing how someone does a job can hurt the employee. If the problem is a small one, they would rather shrug it off than bring it to the worker's attention.
- **They are hopeful the problem will correct itself.** That's wishful thinking. Yet many managers will procrastinate in the hope that the issue will resolve itself or the employee will leave.

The problem with holding back is that the longer you wait, the more difficult it is to get an employee to change. You are also building legal evidence that the problem performer can use in court to claim that any serious actions you might take—like termination for cause—was prompted by some concern other than the employee's behavior. After all, it had been tolerated for a considerable time.

Communicate Openly, Directly, Honestly

If you are to encourage behavioral changes, you have to practice a five-step communication process as a part of your appraisal style:

Step 1. Describe the undesirable behavior. You should have documentation so you can cite specific incidents. Your purpose is to show a discrepancy between the standard set and the current level of performance.

Step 2. Listen to the response. You need to give employees the chance to tell their side of the story or otherwise explain their behavior.

Step 3. Identify the implications. Employees have to know both the effect their behavior is having on workflow and on co-workers' performance. They also have to understand the consequences of continuing the behavior—for instance, being given a warning, denied a raise, or fired.

Step 4. Describe your expectations. What kind of behavior do you want employees to exhibit? If an employee is failing to achieve a key result or outcome, you may want to examine his approach and identify a better way to accomplish the goal. This new way becomes the basis for a new key result or action plan.

Step 5. Get commitment for a change. You want to be sure that employees understand your expectations and buy into the plan to achieve them. To get that cooperation, be sure they feel they've had a voice in forming the plan.

Practice Active Listening

Listening skills play a key part not only in Step 2 of the process just described but throughout it. By now, most managers know that they should repeat what they hear, to demonstrate they are listening, and to use body language to further communicate their interest in what the employee is saying.

But there is more to active listening than that.

Active listening entails a back-and-forth flow of information and comments. To that end, develop a conversational style in which you play the smaller part. You shouldn't dominate the discussion. Remain silent to encourage employees to talk about what's happening in the workplace, problems they have, and how you can help to ensure they achieve key results or outcomes.

Let's say that you ask a question, and Dan, one of your employees, answers, "We've had a real tough time getting Wendy's team to give us the go-ahead because of past problems between our department and hers." Pause for about five seconds, and then make a comment: "I didn't realize that you were encountering personal conflicts in getting the department's support." Then pause again, using silence to get the employee to volunteer additional information.

As you maintain this dialogue, there will be occasions when the employee, whether due to nervousness or personal communication style, or a feeling that he needs to justify actions, seems unable to stop talking. Redirect the employee to a specific topic or get him back on track with a question.

Probe and Question

Critical to effective appraisal interviews is your questioning style. Refine your ability to:

Ask open-ended questions. These are questions that demand more than a "yes" or "no" response. For instance, you might ask a marketer, "How could we develop a more valid customer list?" Or, "Are there ways we can get better placement of our ads in industry publications?" Compare those questions to these: "Can we develop a valid customer list?" Or, "Can we get better placement of our ads in industry publications?" The first set will elicit much better responses.

This is not to suggest that you shouldn't ask some closed-ended questions. Sometimes they can help point up a specific problem, like, "Isn't it true that you completed the data-entry process about a week later than we had anticipated?" But using open-ended questions during appraisal interviews can be more effective in obtaining information about an issue from an employee.

Follow up with pointed questions. Once you ask open-ended questions, probe for greater detail. For instance, "If we worked more closely with customer service and sales to get valid customer lists, what systems would we need to retain the data?" "How could we get help from sales knowing that people in that department always complain about overwork?" "Once we have these lists, how can we maximize their value?"

Combining the Skills: An Example

Let's look at a situation in which a manager needs to be assertive, use good listening skills, and probe with questions to get good information from an employee.

When Dan came in for his quarterly review, Rick, his boss, could see that there was a problem. Usually taciturn, Dan had not stopped chatting about this or that since he had entered. Rick realized that he needed to be assertive and take control of the meeting if he were to get explanations for problems in Dan's performance and use the meeting time productively.

So, in the midst of Dan's story about a problem with ad copy, Rick interrupted. He apologized, then said, "That's very interesting, Dan. It's obviously been a tough year. Let's look, again, at what happened to that database of distributors that was full of information errors. What do you think was the cause?"

Rick designed the open-ended question to focus on the key issue and get a two-way dialogue going—not to mention to put an end to Dan's monologue.

When Dan avoided replying by changing the subject, Rick closed in with a more specific question: "When and how did the error occur?"

Embarrassed, Dan admitted, "I think it occurred when we transferred the list to our new data system."

"How can we prevent a recurrence?" Rick asked, probing further.

Less uncomfortable, Dan began to offer some suggestions for avoiding a repetition of the problem. Rick listened carefully to

Dan's suggestions, saying "uh–huh" to his remarks and nodding and leaning toward Dan to show that he was listening to his ideas. Dan's nervousness slowly disappeared. At one point, he admitted he should have monitored the transfer of records more closely.

Translate into Style

As you look at the three elements of appraisal style—assertiveness, listening skills, and probing ability—you can see that the ideal style is one that holds employees accountable for performance. A manager uses listening and probing skills to find out more about the level of performance of the employee and then takes an assertive approach in evaluating the quality of the work.

But the ideal appraisal style goes beyond that. It's developmental in nature. You, the manager, are more than a taskmaster ensuring that work is done as it should be. Rather, in conducting interviews with employees, you strive to create a supportive environment in which the employee can honestly and openly discuss problems. In it, you both define areas for improvement jointly without demoralizing the employee.

If your style is already like this, then you are fortunate. But don't worry if you're not there yet. It's a style that can be learned. Listening and probing skills are relatively easy to learn and put to use. But most important is the assertive manner, and that comes from within and with practice.

SECTION IV

Follow Up

Chapter Eight

The Year-End Appraisal

"And you know, Willie," said the Agile Manager, "I'm really proud of you for not only taking that first class on financial statements, but then squeezing another one in later in the year."

"Hey, it was on ratios," said William. "I needed it."

The Agile Manager smiled. "You did—and you've put it to good use. I can't believe how 'numberwise' your proposals have become. Anyway, for that item, for which you went way beyond the goal we had set, you get a solid '5.'"

William tried to suppress a smile but couldn't.

The Agile Manager showed him a paper with some calculations done on it and said, "for the year, that means you have an overall average rating of 3.8. That's very good and I'm very happy. And the company is as well." The Agile Manager pointed to another number and said, "That's your bonus for the year."

William's mouth dropped open and seemed unable to speak. "Thank you," he said finally.

The year-end appraisal meeting is similar to the other quarterly meetings in that you discuss personal performance and chart progress toward achieving objectives.

But the year-end appraisal is also the time you give the employee an overall rating for the year. Usually, you'll also award a salary increase, bonus, or another financial incentive.

As mentioned early in the book, the year-end appraisal is best done in two parts. The first meeting is like the others—you discuss performance in relation to goals, pointing to specific incidents when necessary. Employees have a chance to concur or rebut your opinions.

At the second meeting, you offer the employee your rating for the year, and perhaps discuss salary changes or bonus. Then you use the ratings as a springboard to discuss shoring up weak areas or developing new skills in the coming year.

> **Best Tip**
>
> Spend enough time to write a good year-end appraisal. You owe it to yourself and, especially, to your employees.

Start with the Paperwork

The second meeting in this sequence is built around your numerical evaluation of the employee, numbers that are backed up with an explanation in narrative form. The paperwork, at this meeting, is critical, because you use it to justify your rating and share it with employees in a way they can use it to improve performance.

Filling out year-end appraisal forms, however, makes many managers uneasy, because:

- **They worry that narratives won't sufficiently support the ratings they give.** They don't know how much supporting evidence is needed for a defendable rating.

- **They worry that their explanations for the evaluations will be unclear to employees or third parties because they aren't skilled writers.** Some turn to books or computer programs that offer phrases, sentences, even full paragraphs for use in completing assessments. But that often means all the assessments sound alike.

- **They worry that they may wind up in court.** Their narratives may be too vague to counter a charge of discrimination, or they may use language that could be perceived as discriminatory.

These concerns are valid, but they can be overcome using a five-step process:

1. Organize your appraisal writing time.
2. Organize your paperwork.
3. Grade on the basis of weighted goals.
4. Write, write, write.
5. Edit, edit, edit.

Organize Your Appraisal Writing Time

Critical to the process of completing appraisals is allocating sufficient time to do a good job.

Let's put this in perspective. How would you feel if your boss summed up the results of twelve months of your work on an appraisal form she did in fifteen minutes between phone calls?

But managers, whether they have two or twenty-two employees, should set aside sufficient time to think about the ratings and search their memories and files for specific job situations that support the ratings they give, and to write them up.

Organize Your Paperwork

Before you begin analyzing the work your employees have done over the year, gather up your documentation and organize it in a way that makes it easy to rate, and to review in narrative form, their performance.

Organize that information according to the performance factors or objectives to be appraised. Within each stack, you may also want to further organize the information, either by kinds of incidents or quality of performance. Your purpose here is to put all the information in an order that will make it easier to write the appraisal.

Grade on the Basis of Weighted Goals

With your documentation organized, you're ready to rate employees on their performance over the past year. You probably have a number in mind for each objective already, but test it against your documentation. Incidents that occurred early in the year may have escaped your memory.

Your ratings for each goal, while subjective to a certain degree, are thus based heavily on the careful records you have been keeping over the year—critical-incident reports, progress reports, performance memos, and notes from your quarterly appraisal meetings.

At the beginning of the year, remember, you identified the level of difficulty and importance for each goal and used the sum of the products to calculate the percentage weight of each in determining the final rating. (See page 31 to refresh your memory.)

To come up with a final rating, however, you need to rate achievement in each objective or factor. That means you need a rating scale. Try this one, which rates achievement from 1 to 5:

1: The person consistently failed to meet objectives/standards

2: The person's performance was below objectives/standards

3: The person met and sometimes exceeded the objectives/standards

4: The person's performance generally exceeded objectives/standards

5: The person consistently far exceeded the objectives/standards.

Once you've rated each goal, calculating the overall rating is simple. Here's the formula:

(Goal 1 Rating x Percentage Goal 1 x 100) + (Goal 2 Rating x Percentage Goal 2 x 100) + (Goal 3 Rating x Percentage Goal 3 x 100) . . . divided by 100.

Let's say you head customer service for your company. Joe, one of your reps, has five objectives:

1. Handle customer calls with courtesy.
2. Handle calls efficiently.
3. Resolve customer problems successfully.
4. Record customers' names accurately as well as the nature of any complaints for a new database the firm is creating
5. Sell product while providing customer service (upsell).

Joe knows the overall purpose for each goal, and you have measurable standards for them. For example, courtesy is defined both by a lack of customer complaints and occasional management monitoring of calls, efficiency is defined as handling fifty calls a day, resolving problems is defined by an average of .25 call-backs per problem, accuracy is defined as 95 percent accuracy in recording customer details, and the standard for upselling is an average of $1,000 worth of goods sold each month.

At the beginning of the year, you and Joe ranked the importance and difficulty of each goal to come up with an overall weight for each:

Goal	Importance		Difficulty		Total
1. Courteousness	3	x	2	=	6
2. Call efficiency	3	x	3	=	9
3. Complaint resolution	3	x	3	=	9
4. Data entry	3	x	2	=	6
5. Upselling	1	x	3	=	3
			Total:		33

Goal 1: 6 divided by 33 = 18%
Goal 2: 9 divided by 33 = 27%
Goal 3: 9 divided by 33 = 27%
Goal 4: 6 divided by 33 = 18%
Goal 5: 3 divided by 33 = 9%

Based on observation over the year, as well as discussion during appraisal interviews, you give Joe a rating of 4 for his courteous handling of calls, a 3 for the number of incoming calls he processed daily, a 3 for the number of complaints resolved swiftly, a 2 for accuracy, and a 2 for upselling. Let's calculate Joe's year-end rating.

$$\text{Goal 1: } 18\% \times 4 \times 100 = 72$$
$$\text{Goal 2: } 27\% \times 3 \times 100 = 81$$
$$\text{Goal 3: } 27\% \times 3 \times 100 = 81$$
$$\text{Goal 4: } 18\% \times 2 \times 100 = 36$$
$$\text{Goal 5: } 9\% \times 2 \times 100 = 18$$
$$\text{Total: } 288 \text{ divided by 100 or } 2.88$$

What's Joe's final rating for the year? 2.88 or a 3 when rounded off to the nearest full integer.

Joe, overall, met his standards and objectives. You give him a modest raise to cover inflation. Joe has little to quarrel about; he knew the standards and you two discussed his performance and progress over the year.

Moreover, the final appraisal is defendable, as long as goals reflect key behaviors or tasks and the ratings for each goal are supported by information accumulated during the year.

Write, Write, Write

With ratings in hand, you're ready to write out, in narrative form, the basis for them. Write a paragraph for each goal that explains how you arrived at the rating. Along with the form, you may want to include a summary statement about the employee's performance during the year.

If you use our form (page 32), you'll likely need more space than it provides. Attach additional sheets of paper to the form.

Don't try to get everything perfect in the first draft. If you have structured your time smartly, you should have an opportunity to review what you have written.

Here are some points to keep in mind as you prepare your first draft:

Be as specific as possible. Use the active voice, not the passive voice. The passive voice can cloud who did what. For example, rather than say, "The project was done adequately," say, "John did the project adequately."

Further, in describing what an employee did, be as precise as possible. Avoid empty phrases like "maintains good production records" or "caused a significant loss in time," or "behaves professionally." After all, what are "good production records"? What is "significant"? How do you define "professional behavior"?

Instead, note how an employee's production records are 90 percent accurate, or how another worker caused a 50 percent loss in project time, or still another "demonstrates professional behavior by always arriving on time and willingly working through lunch to complete critical projects."

The more exact you are in describing an employee's behavior, the clearer your assessment will be to both the employee and any others who read the assessment—including a court of law if the employee contests the review.

Focus on those incidents that are not subject to interpretation or argument—in other words, the most defendable situations. If you have organized your notes as suggested, these are the critical incidents you placed on the top of the stack of paper relating to each goal. Keep the other information on file in the event you need it to justify your assessment further.

Compare the employee's performance to the standards or goals set. Don't compare the employee's performance to another worker's. Even if you have people with the same goals, such comparison means little. Furthermore, problems can arise between workers if word gets out about the assessment.

However, where a standard is applicable to all employees within the department, and where all employees have met or exceeded that standard except one employee, use this fact to counter the problem performer's argument that the standard is too high.

Use the language of the goals to show a clear relationship between the work done, goals, and rating given. Let's say that you set as a standard that the employee would "build better communications with customers." In writing the appraisal, you might say, "Nina has increased communications with customers by visiting customers' facilities regularly, setting up a program to survey customers on a monthly basis, and . . ."

Edit, Edit, Edit

After you have completed the forms, put them aside for a few hours or days if time allows. Then go back over them. Cross out unnecessary words and replace jargon with language that any manager—not just one from your discipline—would understand.

Ensure legality by making sure that everything written is logical and specific and relates to actual behaviors or tasks critical to doing the job.

Sample Year-end Evaluation

The sample that follows reflects the work done over a year by a customer service rep, Joe, whom you met a few pages back. You and Joe set five goals at the beginning of the year, only two months after he joined your team.

Note that the evaluation points up not only Joe's strengths but his weaknesses and the discussions you and he have had to address those shortcomings in his performance.

To: Human Resources
From: Manager Tito Smith
Re: Assessment, Joe Rosen, 2002

Goal #1: Handle customer calls with courtesy. Rating: 4.
Joe handles customer calls with courtesy, extending himself to find answers to customer questions although he is new to the firm and still not completely familiar with the products we offer. On several occasions, I have seen him reach for our catalog to answer questions or to identify products for customers who want to put through an order but don't have the catalog handy. In addition, no customer has ever complained about Joe.

Goal #2: Handle calls efficiently. Rating: 3.
Joe handles calls efficiently, meeting our standard of 50 calls every day. I've monitored his calls and I have found him very focused without rushing customers.

Goal #3: Resolve customer problems successfully. Rating: 3.
Joe works hard to handle any problems that arise with customer orders. Although he has only been with the firm a little over a

---

year, he has identified some sources of information within the structure on whom he relies for help in expediting delivery. Once he has a new delivery date, Joe follows up with customers per policy to let them know when they can expect their orders. Joe's callback ratio is .23 per problem, which meets standards.

Goal #4: **Record customers' names accurately as well as the nature of any complaints for a new data base the firm is creating. Rating: 2.**
Joe has problems with entering data into our new data base because he has never used a system like ours before. On several occasions, he has categorized complaints incorrectly, creating embarrassing follow-up situations with customers. Joe and I have discussed the problem, and he has asked if he can be given another orientation on the system. Now that he has worked with it a while, he feels that he would benefit more from such an orientation. This may be the case. Joe's peers have not had the same problems with the system, but they worked with the earlier system upon which this system was based. As we've discussed, his accuracy rating, at 81 percent, needs to improve significantly.

Goal #5: **Sell products while providing customer service. Rating: 2.**
Joe doesn't have the familiarity with products that his peers have, and consequently he isn't able to upsell easily. He fell short of the $1,000-per-month goal in ten months out of twelve. He will check customer queries about products in our catalog if he is asked, but he still isn't knowledgeable enough about the product line to make suggestions himself. This knowledge may come in time, but he and I have agreed that during breaks over the first quarter of next year he will spend time with our product engineers and sales people to learn more about the systems used by our customers.

Summary: Joe has met and sometimes exceeded the objectives he and I have set for the year. Consequently, he deserves an overall rating of 3 for the year. The two areas where he falls short of meeting standards—Goals 4 and 5—are likely due to his newness to the company; additional training should remedy the problems.

I'll monitor his performance in these two areas closely next year to determine if he needs extra help to master use of the new data entry system and contribute more to our upselling effort.

Close the Appraisal Process

Not many organizations have a senior manager review appraisals before they are shown to employees. But most ask for advance information about the ratings given. They'll review documentation only when there is a question about a rating being either too high or too low.

Unless the rating seems way out of line, most companies accept managers' evaluations, although managers may be asked to give additional thought to the ratings. If this happens to you, increase your credibility by pulling additional supporting evidence from your personnel files.

Finally, you show written appraisals to employees in the second meeting, and have them sign off.

Since you and your employees have been meeting throughout the year to discuss performance, and you've worked together to determine the impact of the goals set on the final weighted average rating, sharing your ratings should be a formality, right?

Not always.

An employee may suddenly become aware of the impact on salary of the grade or rating given, or realize that the assessment will become a part of his permanent personnel record, and he may question the assessment or even refuse to sign the document. And we're not just talking about marginal performers concerned about job security. Stars whose ratings aren't as high as expected may balk, too.

Faced with disagreement over ratings, don't compromise to avoid litigation. However, hear the employee out. There may be cause to reassess the performance. If you do decide to revise what you wrote, edit in the employee's presence to assure him that you have revised the appraisal. If you still feel strongly that your assessment is correct as is, then say so and provide evidence for your case.

That's usually enough to quiet most employees. Fortunately, if you have met regularly with your employees and provided ongoing feedback, maintained documentation about performance, and used that documentation to prepare logical arguments for your assessments, most staff members will acknowledge the fairness of your assessment by signing the form.

'I Won't Sign'

No matter how well you have handled meetings with marginal employees, they may refuse to cooperate. The most obvious evidence of that will be the staff member's refusal to sign the appraisal form. When this happens, don't become upset. Explain that the signature does not represent agreement with the evaluation. It only signifies that the employee has seen the appraisal, discussed it, and been given a copy.

If an employee wishes to refute your assessment, let her do so in a memo attached to the appraisal when you submit it to the human resources department or put it in your personnel file.

Some employees may not be satisfied with the opportunity to put their argument against your evaluation in writing. They may demand to go over your head, to your boss, to refute your evaluation.

Best Tip

Be specific and precise in writing the year-end evaluation. Write, 'Met sales quota of $350,000,' not, 'Is a good salesperson.'

Tell them to feel free to do so. Even offer to bring your boss and the employee together. As one manager found, the more willing you seem to let the employee meet with your boss, the less willing the employee may be to take advantage of the offer.

The employee in this case wasn't a marginal performer. Her rating wasn't as high as she expected, and she had obtained a higher rating the year before by demanding to go over her supervisor's head. She intended to do it again with her new supervisor.

But to her surprise, the supervisor wasn't concerned at all. She pointed to the documentation that justified her evaluation and reminded the employee that she would have to share that documentation with her boss if the employee went over her head. Then she asked the employee to call the boss within a day or so to resolve the issue.

The manager's self-assurance was disconcerting to the employee, who withdrew her request.

However the meeting with the marginal employee ends, prepare a written record of it and any subsequent meetings you have in which you discuss performance.

One final note: If you eventually terminate the employee, do so with respect. Employees treated with disdain are more likely to sue, charging that the poor treatment is proof of a discriminatory attitude toward them.

You are not done yet. The appraisal is a tool for measuring employee performance and determining a reward for results accomplished. But it's also for identifying weak areas that require coaching and counseling over the next year.

Thus, besides getting your employee's signature on the appraisal forms, use this meeting with the employee to begin planning a program of employee development. We'll cover that next.

The Agile Manager's Checklist

✔ Get away from distracting phone calls and other interruptions to complete appraisal forms.

✔ Organize supporting evidence by goals, with the strongest documentation on the top.

✔ Wherever possible, use numbers to support a grade, whether it is a dollar savings or productivity gain, efficiency rating, or what have you.

✔ Plan ahead how you will react to a refusal to sign off on the appraisal.

Chapter Nine

Create an Employee-Development Plan

" . . . and I'm sorry I took it poorly. I've had a rough few months."
Manuel looked genuinely contrite; Wanda could see how hard it
was for him to apologize.

"You've done great since our last meeting," said Wanda warmly.
"You met every deadline and you and William seem to be getting
along."

"It's been hard for me. Maybe I'm a little bit jealous. I think I still
could use some help in that area—it's hard for me to get people to
do what I need them to do, even when it would benefit them and
the company."

"I used to be known as an extremely prickly person," admitted
Wanda. "That's probably no surprise to you or the others. I felt I
had to be that way to get ahead—especially in some of the companies I worked for. Sometimes you can get what you want by
being snappish, but ultimately people get tired of you and plain
don't cooperate. I had to learn some new skills."

"What did you to?" asked Manuel.

"I went to a human-relations class. It helped me a lot. Each
week they teach you a few skills about getting along with people
or being more effective at work. You practice them the following

week, and then you talk about how well they worked in the next class. It worked wonders with me. Plus I got used to standing up in front of people and talking."

Manuel asked eagerly, "Can I take it—I mean will the company pay for it if I do?"

"Our HR department has similar classes. Why don't you see what they're offering, then compare it to what else is available? I'm sure we can pay for it if you commit to taking it and improving."

"Oh, you can bet I will. I'll sign in blood right now."

Wanda laughed along with Manuel. "That's not necessary," she said.

At the same meeting in which you share your year-end written appraisal of an employee, lay the groundwork for the next year's performance by working out an employee-development plan.

Too often at this meeting, managers talk only about the financial consequences of the employee's performance—the salary increase—and just pay lip service to the developmental side of the appraisal process. But the end-of-year meeting is an excellent time to discuss skill weaknesses evident in the employee's previous year's performance and create action plans to strengthen these areas.

Employee-development is for strong performers, too. If an employee has consistently exceeded expectations and done so for several years, she is probably frustrated with the lack of opportunities for promotion or new challenges. This is the time, then, to discuss training programs she can use to develop skills that could lead to advancement.

This meeting shouldn't be the only time during the year that you address these issues. At every quarterly review, be ready to work out development programs with employees to minimize any shortcomings responsible for their falling behind in the goals set.

At the development meeting, however, most of the time should be spent discussing how the worker can improve performance or develop skills that will enable him to advance to a position of greater responsibility.

If opportunities for advancement do not exist within your organization, or are of little interest to the employee, then you may want to discuss new assignments that would challenge the employee. Or if the employee is not interested in new responsibilities, discuss ways he or she can operate more independently.

Best Tip

Keep employees challenged. It's one of the best motivators you have—often even better than money.

Put on Your Coaching Cap

After the employee has read and signed the appraisal form, discuss ways to maximize strengths while minimizing weaknesses. Prepare a personal development plan with the employee that will make it easier to achieve next year's goals.

Start by identifying goals not met and determine why they weren't met (or why the employee did not "consistently meet expectations"). Identify a skill that should be strengthened or knowledge gap that should be closed.

Most employees want to do good work and have the ability to do so. When results are mediocre and employees don't work at the level you know they can, then something is interfering. Among likely causes to consider:

Stress. At times, outside pressures interfere with employees' day-to-day efficiency. Sometimes it is the demands of the workplace. There's no question that today's leaner work environments demand more work from fewer employees, adding to work stress levels.

Introducing new technology, without adequate training, can also create high stress levels.

Unclear priorities. This is as much your problem as it is an employee's. Yes, he should have asked questions to verify assumptions about what tasks should get top priority. But in setting the standards or goals, you should have raised the issue of priorities with the employee to ensure you agreed which took precedence.

Poor time or task management. Some employees are more adept than others at organizing their responsibilities into manageable tasks. Those who lack this skill can feel overwhelmed when they get multiple assignments, each of equal importance.

Good time management isn't a matter of attitude. It's a matter of skills. And those who lack the ability to organize and budget their time effectively need training in setting priorities, planning, and managing time.

Best Tip
Provide training in time management for those who need it. It's the foundation for accomplishing most tasks.

Confusion about what was expected. The employee signed off on the goals at the start of the previous year but had no clear idea about what she was supposed to be doing. You assumed that she would know what you meant, but you both had different conceptions of the tasks involved in achieving the outcome.

If this was the cause of a performance problem during the previous year, then you and the employee need to agree, as a part of an employee-development plan, to discuss each goal more fully, and to periodically discuss progress toward it. That will ensure confusion doesn't recur.

Oversupervision or undersupervision. When you oversupervise, employees may feel thwarted, unable to pursue their ideas without clearing them with the "boss." Over time, employees adopt an "I do just what I'm told, nothing more" attitude. Once you've set goals with employees, stand back and let them work. They'll surprise you.

If the problem is undersupervision, employees may not know

how to do what they are expected to accomplish. Let them know you stand ready to help.

Interpersonal conflicts. The conflict may be between your employee and another employee or your employee and another supervisor. When a third person is an obstacle to achieving a goal or a critical outcome for your department, arrange for your employee to learn new interpersonal skills to resolve the conflict.

Once you and your employee have identified the cause of any problem performance during the past year, ask yourselves, "How can we prevent a recurrence? How can we create a developmental plan that will give you a better chance of achieving your goals?"

Training is an obvious solution to most skill deficiencies. However, it isn't the sole answer. In some instances, it may not even be the most effective solution. Coaching and counseling employees in their weak areas may be a more productive action. Maybe the solution is simply a matter of your being more accessible to employees. You can provide mentoring or help them think through tough situations.

Enrich the Job

For employees who show promise, your mutual goal is to answer the question, "What can we do to help you accomplish more?"

You don't have to have a vacancy in your department to discuss with somebody opportunities to grow and advance. Talk about training opportunities that will increase the person's "employability," important coinage in today's world of work.

Best Tip

Instead of sending employees out for more training, try being more accessible. It may achieve your ends faster and cheaper.

Ask, "What would you like to learn? What additional skills

would you like to have? What can the company do to prepare you in the event that job X opens up in the department?"

Maybe there is a team project that the employee would like to become involved in. Or, if the individual isn't a team player, there may be a project he can pursue independently as one of the goals for the upcoming year.

Maximize Their Strengths

Developing employees should be part of your game plan as manager. The more effective workers are, the easier your job becomes.

Start by doing your best to use the strengths employees have to the fullest, rather than worrying about minor weaknesses. Your numbers whiz, for example, may be the messiest person in the office. Don't beat your head against a wall trying to make her a neat freak. It'll never happen.

Instead, put her in charge of the tasks that she does best and more efficiently than anyone else.

This doesn't mean you adapt the job to the individual. A job is a set of tasks that need to be accomplished. A customer service rep has to answer phone calls, for example, even if he lacks social graces. That's when you need to train.

Put people in new jobs if you must, or switch tasks with those in other positions. Putting the strengths of your people to use is a juggling act—but that's what a good manager does day in and day out.

Empower Employees

Some employees are neither poor workers nor superstars. And the work they do is routine. But if they are given the opportunity to empower themselves, they can free you to do more of your own work.

Train employees in problem solving and other skills, familiarize them with the broad picture, and communicate department goals and other critical issues. That ensures employees are prepared to make good decisions on their own. They'll enrich their jobs while opening up your schedule for special projects of your own.

Set Development Objectives

The objectives you set in the employee-development plan should be included among the goals you determine for the next year's performance appraisal.

In creating the employee-development plan, don't forget to:

Involve the employee. You won't get buy-in, otherwise. Even if you make its completion critical to next year's performance rating, you're not likely to get employee cooperation if you don't make them a part of the planning process.

Begin at the beginning. The beginning is convincing the employee that there is a skill or knowledge deficiency that must be addressed.

> **Best Tip**
>
> Involve employees in setting developmental objectives. If you don't get buy-in from the start, you're doomed to failure.

You may have to demonstrate the need for a plan by sharing documentation with an employee. If that isn't sufficient, remind her that failing to work toward the developmental objective you've suggested will probably mean failing to meet the objective or standard related to the problem area as well.

Address problems in performance before you look at opportunities to enrich jobs or provide more challenging assignments or a chance for promotion.

Write down goals. Like performance goals, put developmental goals in writing. Add them to the appraisal form.

You should note your responsibility for those development goals in which your participation is critical. Then monitor your own efforts to support employees to determine how you are influencing their performance.

Don't wait until quarterly appraisal interviews to assess whether employees are making progress toward developmental goals. If you're not pleased with the efforts being made to implement the development plan, talk to the employee about what should be done. Remember, accomplishing development goals may ensure accomplishing performance goals.

The Agile Manager's Checklist

✔ Include discussion of developmental needs in the second year-end appraisal meeting.

✔ Use the past year's appraisal to identify skill deficiencies or other performance problems to remedy over the next year.

✔ Don't limit remedial efforts to training. Consider coaching, counseling, or mentoring an employee to turn performance around in specific areas.

✔ Put developmental goals in writing and incorporate them into next year's performance appraisal.

✔ Develop an action plan to improve performance in the future.

Manage Performance Like a Pro

You want productive employees. You want employees who can learn and adapt as their roles change. You want employees who can move in step with your organization as its focus and direction change.

How do you make sure employees keep up as their jobs change? By managing performance.

That is something you do through the appraisal process, of course, but also by coaching employees, counseling problem performers, and mentoring your best people.

Practice Three Essential Skills

Coaching, counseling, and mentoring are all essential management skills. Unfortunately, you often see these three concepts used interchangeably in management textbooks. That creates confusion.

Few managers, further, are skilled at doing any of them well, which makes it hard to learn by observation. Most managers, for example, are uncertain of the various roles involved in each process, the best way of proceeding, and how to avoid problems that may arise.

You've already encountered the concepts of coaching and counseling in this book. As you'll see, however, I'll broaden the concept of each—and introduce you to the power of mentoring.

Coaching. Coaching, in the context of performance management, means bringing the right people onto the team and developing them continually so that they do their jobs better all the time.

Think in terms of baseball, football, or volleyball coaches. They first recruit the right people, assess training and development needs, and work to improve the skills of all. A manager is a coach in just the same way.

As a coach, for instance, one of your jobs is to hire top talent. Then, if at any point people lack the skills they need to do their jobs well, your job is to train them. Analyzing training needs is, in fact, an ongoing responsibility, since skill needs change as the demands of the workplace change.

Besides making sure your employees have the skills they need, as coach you need to ensure they understand the organization's values and mission. Otherwise, your employees may create problems for themselves or for you.

Counseling. All managers must deal with employees who don't meet standards in one way or another. It's best to deal with budding problems as soon as possible through a process called counseling.

Counseling is a four-step process in which you:

1. Alert employees about problems in their work;

2. Make them understand that poor performance cannot be tolerated;

3. Develop an action plan to turn poor performance around;

4. Document discussion to ensure—and to prove—that you made a reasonable effort to help the employee perform well.

Documentation, as discussed throughout this book, is critical to protect you from legal action by disgruntled employees if you have to discipline or terminate.

Mentoring. Mentoring is often confused with coaching. But in the context of the performance-management system advocated here, it refers to coaching the best performers on staff to ensure that their outstanding performance continues.

As a manager in today's leaner organization, you know you have less opportunity to give big financial rewards or offer promotions. Mentoring may not replace these plums or guarantee a talented worker will stay on indefinitely in your department, but it gives you a means to demonstrate to top performers that you recognize their worth.

There's even something in it for you. In your role as mentor, you identify assignments that will give your best performers the opportunity to grow beyond their current jobs. Some will be mundane tasks of your own. Others will be tasks you need help to get done. In either case, assigning these projects to your best performers ensures they learn new skills while freeing you to take on more rewarding, high-visibility tasks.

If you mentor those who truly deserve the opportunity, you will not only motivate the individuals you have chosen to mentor but also demonstrate to the rest of your organization that you care about your staff members.

Coaching, counseling, and mentoring may all seem very simple. In fact, most books on coaching or counseling make these two processes seem extremely easy. Likewise, any discussion about mentoring often makes the act of mentoring, even traditional mentoring in which the focus is solely on career matters, seem a breeze.

Not so. Problems can arise with any one of them. And because failing to coach, counsel, or mentor employees adequately can add to your challenges and ultimately make the appraisal process more difficult, let's look at each of them in detail and discuss the kinds of problems you might encounter and how to handle them.

Coach Like a Pro

Coaching is something you begin from the first day an employee arrives on the job. It's best done systematically, and not in a haphazard fashion. Aim to coach each of your people, one on one, at least once a month.

Many managers argue they don't have the time to coach on a regular basis. But ask yourself, "What does it cost in time or money if my employees don't have a clear view of operating priorities or plans, or lack critical skills, or are encountering problems that impede progress?"

I can predict your answer: The cost in time and money will be considerably more than the time you'd spend coaching. In other words, coaching is preventative maintenance.

While coaching mostly involves one-on-one meetings, bear in mind that it can also take the form of group sessions. The intent of these meetings is the same as one-on-one sessions—to better prepare employees to do their jobs.

Group sessions can thus provide information on action plans, focus on skill-building activities, or remedy small group performance difficulties before they grow beyond control.

Here's how to coach:

Question employees about work in progress. Get information from employees without making them feel as if they are being interrogated.

Do that by asking probing, open-ended questions. Examples: "What's keeping you from doing an even better job than you are now?" Or, "Is there anything we need to talk about?"

Developing the knack of asking such questions in a nonthreatening way helps you uncover problems that may not otherwise come to light, identify a skill deficiency, or discover an employee's interests and aspirations. Getting an employee to reveal aspirations, by the way, allows you to redesign the job and thereby stimulate above-standard performance.

Listen. Probe, but then listen to what is said. A good coach practices "active listening," paying attention not only to the words but to nonverbal signals. Those include posture and moments of silence. Nonverbal signals often say more about how an individual feels than responses to questions raised.

Stay alert to what's happening. Keep lines of communication open. You can perhaps do that best by practicing MBWA (managing by walking around). Jot down casual comments or follow-up thoughts you can discuss during one-on-one meetings you hold with staff members each month.

Train employees. No new hire comes fully qualified to take on the job. Nor do jobs remain the same. Assessing training needs is one of the coach's ongoing responsibilities. Be alert to new abilities staff members need to do their current jobs well, and then provide needed training—or see that it is provided.

Sometimes, training may involve the entire staff. Other times, it is necessary for one or two employees whose jobs have changed. Sometimes, too, you need to train to strengthen a particular skill for one staff member.

Give feedback. There is no such thing as too much feedback about job performance. Praise for a job well done reinforces that behavior and increases the likelihood of its continuation. Suggestions for improvement tell employees you think they are capable of doing better.

Are you coaching well? Ask yourself these questions:

- Am I keeping my staff members informed on how well they are doing on the job?
- Do I offer frequent insights so employees can make the best decisions?
- Do I communicate in a way that makes my messages clear to my team members?

- Do I communicate my trust and confidence in my employees?
- Are my staff members clear about project priorities?
- Are both department goals and organization mission clear to staff? If they see conflicts, have I taken the time to resolve them in employees' minds?
- When I meet with staff members, do I ask their thoughts as to how we can improve operations, as well as what I might do to help them accomplish their tasks?
- Do I seek out information from staff about obstacles or barriers they are encountering in doing their jobs and how I might help them?
- Do I give my staff my full attention when we sit down one-on-one to talk?
- When I talk to staff, do I listen for tone as well as words?
- Do I keep a record of coaching sessions?

The last question is worthy of further discussion. Keep notes of your coaching sessions. Documenting them is as important as documenting evaluation sessions. A memo to yourself may be sufficient. If the information is critical to the employee's development, then share the memo with him or her.

Alternatively, you may want to develop a form like the one shown on the next page. After each meeting, jot down key points discussed during the coaching session. These might include training needs and plans, solutions to problems, answers to routine questions, scheduling items, or insights and ideas shared.

Handle Problems in Coaching

Through conversations with many managers, I have identified some of the problems you may encounter as a coach. Let's look at these and how you can avoid them.

Problem: Failing to prepare new hires. Aware of a new hire's skill deficiencies during interviewing, we often plan to close that gap with training once the individual is at work. But by the

Employee Coaching Form

Employee:
Date:

What does the employee think he or she did well?

What could the employee have done better? Were expectations clear?

Are there obstacles to the employee doing his work? If so, what action plans did we agree on to overcome these?

Are there skill gaps? What training needs exist that would enable the employee to do his job better? What training does the employee want?

time the person arrives, our first thought is to get the individual
to work. We don't undertake a more formal training needs assessment or clarify our expectations to get the employee off to a
good start. Worse, we fail to spend time talking with the new
hire about the group's mission or objectives as they relate to the
whole organization's strategy.

Solution: Conduct a training-needs assessment, follow through
on skill-building exercises, and make sure new hires understand
the organization's mission and what it takes to succeed.

Problem: Making promises you can't keep. When coaching,
there is the danger of tying a request for greater productivity to
a promise of a promotion or big raise or higher job grade that
you can't guarantee. But a broken promise can undo the positive
work relationship that coaching sessions create.

Solution: Be careful that your enthusiasm doesn't get out of
control and cause you to make offers you can't live up to.

Problem: Managing with a heavy hand and forgetting that
you have to win the support of employees.

Solution: Understand that coaching is a management style
that requires you to communicate openly and honestly, respect
each other, and recognize outstanding performance, among other
things.

If you are known more as an autocrat than as a team leader
with a willingness to share leadership with members, employees
will initially laugh at your efforts at coaching. You will have to
work to gain their trust.

Problem: Undermining employee self-esteem. Some managers forget that one of the purposes of coaching is to demonstrate your belief that employees are capable of meeting your
expectations and much more.

Solution: Watch your language. Avoid "never" or "always" if
it suggests that the employee "never" does such and such correctly or, along the same lines, "always" does such and such wrong.

Problem: Failing to follow up.

Solution: Do what you say you will do. If you promise to arrange for training, intervene with another manager, remove roadblocks to good work, or what have you, then you need to do just that. You should be ready to support your employee.

Problem: Placing the blame. Some managers blame employees for 100 percent of the problem.

Solution: Open your eyes. Consider the possibility that you are part of the problem. For instance, don't go into a counseling session with a preconceived notion that the employee alone is responsible for performance difficulties.

Counsel Like a Pro

Your role as coach focuses primarily on your employees' knowledge and skill. When one of your workers is doing well, your goal is to help him or her build on job strengths. When the employee isn't doing well, your intent is to further clarify what's expected, help the employee acquire the knowledge and skill needed to improve job performance, and step in and address any external obstacles that may be impeding performance.

There are times, however, when coaching just won't work. After you've made several attempts to solve the performance problem to no avail, then it becomes evident that something other than lack of knowledge or skill is behind the problem. At this point, you need to move from being coach to being counselor.

There are obvious reasons to engage in counseling. For instance, a poor performer is often half as productive as an average worker. Bringing this person up to average productivity can improve your department's performance considerably.

Besides, left to fester, performance problems can ultimately take up as much as 50 percent of your time in meetings with the poor performer and with human resources people to initiate termination proceedings. There's no time to do your own work, which includes coaching the rest of the staff.

Further, other employees will lose respect for you and begin to doubt the fairness of your evaluations. Either their performance will decline or they will move on to another company. Worse, some managers have told me that their failure to confront poor performers has sometimes had an effect on their own self-confidence. They may use worries about the legal consequences or time commitment as reasons for ignoring the problem, but in time they begin to think less of themselves as managers.

Some fears managers have are understandable. Unless you have a clear idea about how to counsel a marginal performer, you may have cause to worry about losing control of the discussion, particularly if the employee becomes emotional and starts to cry or shout. And there is a real danger of landing in court if counseling isn't done correctly.

The secret to good counseling is accomplishing the following objectives during a one-on-one interview:

- Get the employee to agree that there is a need for a change in quality of performance.
- Identify the nature of the problem in the employee's performance.
- Reach agreement on the specific actions that the employee will take to improve performance.
- Follow up regularly with the employee to ensure that he or she is reaching the goals you both have set.

To reinforce continued improvement, recognize efforts by the employee to improve performance.

Of these four steps, the most difficult may be the first. For counseling to work, the employee must agree that yes, indeed, a problem in performance exists and that the employee is responsible.

Earlier, we discussed the need for documenting performance.

Documenting counseling sessions is critical. Not only must your documentation describe the nature of the problem but also how the problem affects the performance of the department as a whole.

A secret in gaining employee agreement lies in demonstrating a willingness to hear the employee's explanation. To prompt a response, you might say, "Tell me about it," "Is my understanding correct?" or "Is there more I need to know about what happened?"

If there are reasons for the problem beyond the performance of the employee, then the matter should be over.

If you have doubts about the employee's explanation, share them then and there or offer to look further into the matter and get back to the employee. Often, if the employee is stalling, either approach will be sufficient to get the employee to say something like, "Gee, I guess I could have handled the situation better," or, "I might be responsible—a little—for what happened. What would you have wanted me to do?"

Getting buy-in to the solution is important to the success of the counseling session, but perhaps even more important is clarifying the cause of the problem.

Many different situations lie behind problem performance. The cause might be due to stress within or outside the workplace, unclear priorities (more attributable to the manager than employee), or poor time or task management on the employee's part. Personal problems also create work-related problems, distracting employees from the work and making them unproductive and maybe argumentative and uncooperative.

Whatever the cause, once you identify it, you are better able to develop an action plan to turn the performance around.

But remember: That action plan works only if the employee has played a major role in its development. Helping to create the plan increases the likelihood of buy-in to the solution.

Once the plan is in action, monitor the employee's performance. Meet at set times to review progress.

To measure yourself as a counselor, ask yourself these questions:

■ Am I making allowances for some poor performer's work? Consequently, is performance slipping within the department?

■ Am I using my busy schedule as an excuse to avoid confronting the performance problem?

■ When I meet with an employee to discuss her poor performance, am I clear about the purpose of the meeting?

■ Do I describe clearly the performance that troubles me, pointing to documentation I've maintained?

■ Do I plan the one-on-one meeting in advance, even preparing a list of questions I might be asked—and my answers—to ensure I maintain the focus of the meeting?

■ Do I give an employee in counseling the opportunity to tell her story without interruption?

■ Do I allow the employee to identify several alternative solutions to the problem and to share her feelings about each of the alternatives before settling on a single solution to the problem?

■ Do I demonstrate to the employee that I am truly listening to her explanation by paraphrasing what she has said?

■ Do I use open-ended questions to stimulate the discussion?

■ Do I keep from making judgements about the employee, like calling her "lazy," "difficult to work with," or a "loser"?

■ Do I refer employees with personal problems to the employee assistance program or human resources department or some community program to enable them to address the non-work-related part of the problem? At the same time, do I make clear to the employee that having a personal problem is no excuse for failure to do her job well?

■ Am I clear about the specific work that must be improved?

■ Did I offer to help to ensure the change?

■ Am I ready to meet with the employee as agreed in the improvement plan?

A "no" to one or more of the questions here could create problems in counseling.

Avoid Counseling Mistakes

The biggest mistake you can make with poor performance is, of course, ignoring the problem. If you allow the problem to continue over a long period of time—some managers admit to years—addressing the problem at some late date becomes fraught with legal ramifications.

It also makes other actions difficult. For instance, let's assume you have a problem performer who applies for a promotion. He's not doing his current job well as is, and you have no intention of letting him be paid more for not doing another, higher-graded position. So you turn him down and choose another employee—perhaps someone newer in the company—for the position.

Surprise! The poor performer sues for discrimination, claiming either a gender, age, or racial bias. Since you have never addressed the issue of performance, raising it at this point is unlikely to justify your action. What would you tell the court?

Sometimes, employees reach the warning stage yet claim they had no knowledge about a problem. In some instances, it is an excuse. In others, unfortunately, it is because the manager never made clear the nature of the problem and the consequences if they did nothing about the situation.

That's why it is essential that, in counseling employees, you be very specific about the existence of the problem, its nature, and, most important, the consequences if the employee does nothing to remedy the situation. Further, you need to document this session and share a copy with the problem performer, including the agreed-on action plan to address the problem. Documenting incidents that justify counseling will make it easier to prove a problem does, indeed, exist.

And don't forget that involving employees in setting the standards by which performance is measured minimizes disagreement over standards. If other employees have similar standards and met them, you can remind the employee of that fact.

If, in defending his performance, the employee argues that standards are too high, and this is the first time he has raised this issue, you can use your documentation to point out the obvious: At no point in setting standards did the employee raise the issue.

There are some communication mistakes to avoid during counseling as well. For instance, don't dominate the discussion. Practice the 20/80 rule—speak only 20 percent of the time and listen 80 percent of the time.

Focus, too, on the problem. Don't bring emotions into the discussion by dwelling on how the problem performance is making you feel. Stick to the facts. You may understand how the problem could have developed, you may even empathize with the employee if it stems from personal problems, but you have to remain objective. If your staff member senses that you are sympathetic, there's less chance for a change in behavior.

And don't dictate a solution to the employee. As mentioned, the employee must be truly involved in creating the plan for it to work.

Finally, spend sufficient time identifying the nature of the problem. Don't think you can save time by jumping quickly into the problem-solving phase. Indeed, any employee being counseled needs to feel that his manager is willing to give the needed time to address the problem. Show you care.

Mentor Like a Pro

Much is written about mentoring, but the focus is usually on career advancement. There's an equally valuable purpose for mentoring that's written about much less: To keep talented top performers motivated and to shorten the learning curve for skilled newcomers.

Mentoring is often confused with coaching because one of the functions of a mentor is to coach the protégé. While mentoring uses many of the same techniques as coaching, it goes beyond coaching in that you share your experience, wisdom, and political savvy to enable excellent performers to take on tasks beyond their job titles.

Mentors have four roles:

Role model. Like the original "Mentor," Telemachus's teacher in *The Odyssey,* managerial mentors should serve as models of good behavior.

Coach. As mentors, managers help their protégés better understand the organization's culture, vision, and politicking. This ensures that protégés direct their efforts correctly and sidestep the political traps that could derail career advancement.

Serve, then, as a sounding board for your protégé's ideas and offer insights into how your protégé can make her ideas a reality. When the protégé makes a mistake, have the patience to explain the error and offer not only a more effective way to handle the situation but also time to remedy the error and get her back on track.

Broker. When you act as mentor, you share your contacts with your protégé. Make your network of colleagues, peers, and professional acquaintances available to her.

Advocate. As a mentor, you are chief cheerleader for your protégé, giving her the chance to show others her capabilities.

Managers have often asked me why they should be mentors. Let's look at the value of mentoring for you:

Faster learning curves. When you mentor a new hire, you give the person your personal attention, putting that employee on a high-performance fast track. There's no wasted time in learning how the organization operates.

Increased communication. New people get insights into corporate values immediately. Longer-term employees learn about shifts in focus and direction as soon as they occur. Both gain this knowledge from your ongoing communications.

Reduced turnover. If there is one critical value of mentoring top talent, it is its use in reducing turnover at a time when new recruits may be hard to find.

When you have a talented worker, you want that person to stay. You often can't offer a retention bonus, but you can demonstrate through extra coaching how much you think that the person can make a major contribution to the organization. If the individual is wise, he or she will recognize that this added attention is more valuable over the long term than the financial compensation of a bonus.

Increased loyalty. Mentoring efforts tell your employees that you care for them beyond their ability to complete today's work. It lets them know that you are as concerned as they are about their employability. This builds loyalty not only to your organization but—perhaps more important—to you.

Better employee performance. Protégés will be motivated to work harder, to take on challenging work, and to operate outside their organizational boxes with direction from you. You can stop a decline in performance as your top people learn that their performance won't get them a quick promotion or big bonus check. Mentoring becomes a reason for your superstars to continue to outperform their peers.

More time for your own work. Yes, when you have protégés to whom you can pass work that you otherwise would have to do yourself, you free yourself to work on other projects, increasing your productivity.

Could you be an excellent mentor? The answer is yes if you can answer "yes" to these questions:

- Do you have strong interpersonal skills?
- Do you have contacts both within and outside the organization that you can share with others?
- Are you willing to acknowledge the accomplishments of others?
- Are you willing to be available to help another advance?

- Are you willing to listen to personal problems?
- Are you open to the ideas of others?
- Are you willing to stand by your protégé in a difficult situation?
- Are you willing to give the time it might take to meet regularly with a protégé as she learns under your tutelage?
- Do you understand your organization well enough to explain its ins and outs to another?
- Are you in a position to offer growth experiences to a protégé?

If you decide to mentor a superstar on your staff, it is often enough to offer him some special assignments that involve a stretch with a promise to lend a hand. But the offer carries with it a promise to be available when your protégé needs advice or counsel. Often, managers offer to mentor an employee then fail to keep their promise to make time for the worker.

So be certain that you will keep your promise to be accessible to the employee. A closed door can leave a superstar disgruntled enough that she seeks another mentor, often in another company.

Sometimes, too, you may choose someone to mentor only to discover in time that you and the protégé can't get along. If the differences in personality are great, then it is better to acknowledge a problem and see if you can arrange for another mentor for the talented employee.

You may also find that you chose poorly—the protégé lacks the abilities he needs and is unable to acquire them. You have tried to give the individual assignments to stretch his skills, but he's failed one time after another. Better to go back to traditional coaching. Find opportunities to help that employee grow in the job, but look for another to pass on those politically sensitive assignments.

Some managers lack strong coaching capability. Rather than build their protégés up, they tear them down with harsh feed-

back. If staff complains that your criticism is extremely negative, rather than seek out a protégé you might want to seek
out a mentor for yourself. You may need help in building the
coaching skills you require to work effectively with your
employees.

Index

Among the Books in the Agile Manager Series™
At your bookseller, or call 888-805-8600 or visit
www.agilemanager.com

The Agile Manager's Guide To
GIVING GREAT PRESENTATIONS
By Jeff Olson

The Agile Manager's Guide To
EXTRAORDINARY CUSTOMER SERVICE
By Susan M. Gage

The Agile Manager's Guide To
GETTING ORGANIZED
By Jeff Olson

The Agile Manager's Guide To
UNDERSTANDING FINANCIAL STATEMENTS
By Joseph T. Straub

The Agile Manager's Guide To
BUILDING AND LEADING TEAMS
By Joseph T. Straub

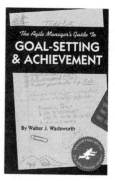

The Agile Manager's Guide To
GOAL-SETTING & ACHIEVEMENT
By Walter J. Wadsworth

The Agile Manager's Guide To
MANAGING IRRITATING PEOPLE
By Joseph T. Straub

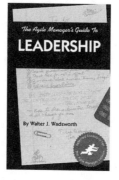

The Agile Manager's Guide To
LEADERSHIP
By Walter J. Wadsworth

The Agile Manager's Guide To
INFLUENCING PEOPLE
By John R. Hook

If you liked this book, try this one:
Coaching to Maximize Performance
($9.95, ISBN 1-58099-016-9)

Widely respected coaches Jack Cullen and Len D'Innocenzo impart secrets of coaching and leadership they learned the hard way. You'll discover how to:

- Tailor your coaching to personality style
- Create a productive motivational environment
- Set goals and communicate expectations clearly
- Develop people to make them more valuable
- Confront poor performers constructively
- Practice hands-on coaching

With new-found coaching skills in hand, you'll easily meet goals, boost overall performance—and expand your value to the organization.

Praise for *Coaching to Maximize Performance:*

"It's about time that Cullen and D'Innocenzo brought their refreshing common sense and trademark motivational spirit to the topic of coaching. If you want tangible, on-the-mark tips to help you develop those intangible qualities we all recognize as true coaching, this is the book."

Tom Ritchey, President, Carlson Learning Company

"For years, I've hired Cullen and D'Innocenzo to help maximize the performance of my people. Their ideas work."

Len Bizzarro, Vice President, Worldwide Marketing, Intergraph

To order this book, call 1-888-805-8600, go to *www.agilemanager.com*, or see your local bookseller.